WHO SAID SHE CAN'T?

WHO SAID SHE CAN'T?

Inspiring stories of pioneering women graduates of IIT Bombay

RASHMI BANSAL

BUSHFIRE PUBLISHERS

Originally published as a coffee table book by the Indian Institute of Technology, Bombay (2022).

Content and formatting by
Bushfire Publishers LLP (2022).

Paperback edition by Bushfire Publishers (2024)
(venture by Rashmi Bansal).
Core House, Off CG Road, Near Parimal Garden
Ahmedabad 380006.

P Book ISBN: 978-81-947679-3-0
E Book ISBN: 978-81-947679-9-2

Cover Design by Pallavi Kapur
Page Design by Jini Anto

Printed at Thomson Press (I) Ltd.

Dedicated to the memory of
Dr. Homi Bhabha

For making India a Science Nation.

DIRECTOR'S NOTE

WHO SAID SHE CAN'T
IIT BOMBAY GEN ZERO WOMEN

PROF. SUBHASIS CHAUDHURI
DIRECTOR, IIT BOMBAY

In the early days of IITs, the engineering profession was considered to be almost a no-go for women. It is worth pondering what a bold step these first-generation women alumnae of our Institute had taken. Ever since it was set up in 1958, IIT Bombay has enrolled extraordinary women students who have gone on to lead very successful and fulfilling lives after graduating from the Institute. This book aims to highlight and applaud their incredible journeys and accomplishments.

IIT Bombay alumna Damini Kumari conducted in-depth interviews with these women as part of a podcast series and Rashmi Bansal then converted it into a coffee table book titled, *Her Story – IIT Bombay Gen Zero Women*. As the stories are of interest to a wider audience, the content is now being published in the form of a paperback.

IIT Bombay has always been at the forefront of the gender equality movement. A book like *Who Said She Can't* is timely and essential. While the world slowly takes strides toward gender equality, there is still a significant divide in many fields, including within STEM in academia. I hope that this book will ignite passion in young minds across the globe, especially young girls, and that they will find their future at IIT Bombay.

American poet Robert Frost once wrote,

> "TWO ROADS DIVERGED IN A WOOD, AND I—
> I TOOK THE ONE LESS TRAVELED BY,
> AND THAT HAS MADE ALL THE DIFFERENCE."

Indeed. The women of *Who Said She Can't* took the tough and difficult roads ahead of them and came out stronger and more successful. And that makes their stories truly inspirational.

I hope readers will enjoy reading the book.

ABOUT THE BOOK

IIT BOMBAY GEN ZERO WOMEN

It is a matter of immense pride to the Institute that thousands of women have graduated from IIT Bombay since it was set up in 1958. This book was conceived to celebrate the achievements of the women who graduated from IIT Bombay in the first three decades of its existence. Each of the women profiled has made stellar contributions to her chosen areas - research, business, education, technology, public service, and more.

The primary goal of the book is to make these accomplishments visible to the IIT Bombay alumni community, and the rest of the world. It documents their lives – from the successes and challenges they faced on campus, to their subsequent professional and personal trajectories. The book also explores how their education and networking experiences on campus, especially the personal connections with hostel batchmates, enriched their lives and made them the strong and powerful women they are today.

The content of Who Said She Can't was originally published as a coffee book titled *Her Story - IIT Bombay Gen Zero Women,* for private circulation. The initiative was made possible by a generous grant from Renu and D.C. Agrawal (IIT Bombay Class of '69, Mechanical Engineering). The paperback edition has been released to take these stories to a wider audience, to encourage and inspire newer generations of brilliant and diverse minds, especially young women, to take up careers in STEM.

We are certain they will make IIT Bombay their first and only choice of college, and blaze the same trails set by the women who came before them.

AUTHOR'S NOTE

I did not study at IIT Bombay but feel closely connected to it. 7 of the 22 girls I grew up with attended this institution; 5 of them are featured in this book. Our fathers worked at the Tata Institute of Fundamental Research (TIFR) as scientists, mathematicians, astrophysicists.

Was there something special in the air at the TIFR campus? I think so. We never had a clue about what 'girls cannot do'. IIT was simply the norm. Not getting admission made more news than another TIFR kid - boy or girl - embarking on the IIT journey.

I know now that this was highly unusual. That women who joined IITs in the 70s, 80s, 90s were exceptional in so many ways. Being the lone girl in a class of high-achieving nerds would not have been easy. Yet they persisted, they resisted and they thrived.

I am full of awe and admiration for these pioneering women. And that is why I took up this project, as a labor of love. The world needs to hear the stories of IIT Bombay women, and know of their remarkable achievements. Because if they could do it, so can each of you out there.

Yes, there is a far higher ratio of girls at IIT now. But it's still not a level playing field. So take inspiration from those who have walked the path before you. Forget about 'patriarchy', about 'discrimination'. Aim for excellence in your chosen field, and be a good human being.

That is what the world can learn from this amazing cohort of women.

I celebrate their grit, their intelligence, their confidence and chutzpah.

IIT Bombay, you were lucky to have them!

Rashmi Bansal
March 2024

ACKNOWLEDGEMENTS

Many thanks to **Damini Kumari,** who conducted the interviews on which the profiles are largely based.

(The original interviews are available as a podcast on the IIT Bombay website).

Core team members **Anuradha Narsimhan and Rekha Koita** for their counsel. **Sunita Parasuraman and Shivani Govil** for their ongoing support.

To **Nidhi Mathur, Manjula Mehta and Indraneel Ghosh** for co-ordinating and facilitating this book in countless ways.

Pallavi Kapur for the impactful cover design.

Madhavi Gokhlay for her diligent proofreading.

Jini Anto for her excellent work in laying out the text and photos to create a wonderfully readable book.

Varsha Shah from Rashmi's team for her tireless efforts to tie up all loose ends.

Manish Singh and the team at Thomson Press for ensuring print and paper quality.

To all the women featured for generously sharing their stories and personal photos.

Special thanks to **Dr Bhagwati Prasad** for the touching write-up on his late wife Dr Rinti Banerjee.

To all others at IIT - the Dean, faculty, alumni and in particular the donor who conceived of this project - for their implicit support.

CONTENTS

FOR THE MOST UP-TO-DATE CAREER STATUS OF EACH WOMAN PROFILED, OR TO CONNECT WITH THEM, PLEASE REFER TO LINKEDIN.COM

TO BOLDLY GO WHERE NO WOMAN HAD GONE BEFORE...

Joining as Professor of Practice, 35 years after being a student at IITB

JOSH MACHINE

I am happiest when meeting people, solving problems and volunteering for causes.

Early Life

I grew up in Ahmedabad in a home with working parents and remember being a 'speak when you are spoken to' person until I was around 11, when I met some outgoing seniors at school and wanted to be like them. I went about working on my confidence and my oh-so-South-Indian accent. After a year of modelling myself on these seniors, it was almost a metamorphosis. This gave me the belief that I could be anything I want to be as long as I wanted it enough, and it has held me in good stead always.

Appa was a geologist with a transferable quasi-government job and Amma was a school-teacher, who stayed strictly away from the school her children went to. So as long as I wasn't following in the footsteps of my slightly laidback, mischievous older brother, life was good. Of course, being the nerd and every teacher's first-bencher pet set the bar high for the unsuspecting younger brother who unfortunately had to follow me. Life came easy – math, books, friends, the game of lagori, train trips to meet relatives – all enjoyed with great gusto.

There was never a doubt in my head that I was going to be an engineer, not because I loved building things, duh, that was all my family spoke of. If you were good at math and science, why would you not be one? Squirming at the sight of blood ruled out the other prevalent career option, quite simply.

I think Amma had more ambition for me than I had for myself, she had been quite the rebel in her growing up years. My strong-willed, gregarious mother has always been my role model. Appa, on the other hand, had

DR. ANURADHA NARASIMHAN

B.Tech, Civil Engineering, 1990

Professor of Practice and Head DS School of Entrepreneurship, IITB; Director, Africa Improved Foods; Director, Frontier Nutrition, Bangladesh

implicit faith in me and quietly, he was the wind beneath my wings. He said, "If not IIT, you can go someplace else - you just have to do well at whatever you do!"

The curly-haired, intense look

The little band of 20 – who studied Science in XI/XII in this small Ahmedabad school – have gone on to give me lifelong friendships but back then we were collaborative competitors. We paced each other, we set goals, we taught and supported each other, and I am grateful to this one friend who I beat in the Board Exams but who beat me hollow in JEE ranks – that clearly raised the bar and fuelled ambition. I had a whole set of teachers rooting for me, and I needed to do the world proud, and yet I don't remember it as the kind of pressure I see in today's world.

Life at IIT Bombay

I was a wide-eyed freshie who took a train from a sheltered home in a small town to Big, Bad Bombay. After Amma left me and went home, my first realization was, "Hey, there is no 9 pm curfew, I actually have a 24-hour day to do as I please". I had long curly hair in pigtails which got cut short rather early – I told Amma I was missing classes in my quest to comb my hair. But it was just a rite of passage, from nerdy schoolgirl to smart young woman.

First graduation, with IITB friends

The gender ratio of my batch was 300 guys to 9 girls, in Civil Engineering 29 to 1. I think this unnatural proportion was overwhelming, and it wasn't easy for either gender to make the first move. I decided to put my hand out first and slowly but surely made friends, not just with my class but the entire batch. Since then, I have always made it my job to be included in groups – to contribute and to belong, thank you IITB for giving me the practice. When I came back to IIT as a professor, seeing the multi-storey Hostel 10 and meeting the 1 in 4 IITian women has totally warmed my heart.

I remember being the average on Prof. Dipan Ghosh's first Physics quiz – got 6 out of 25. It kind of told you whether you would make it in the tech world or not. I wasn't too bummed; was just happy to do everything else that IITB offered. Tried my hand at Mountaineering, HAM Radio, Treasure Hunts, crossies, even representing IITB at Inter-IIT basketball. Some of my favorite hangouts other than hostel messes were the SAC, H8 Chinese corner,

Celebrating brother's 50th birthday

Staff C, Vadilal Samosas. Give me chai and conversations over absolutely anything else.

I thrived in leadership roles - Positions of Responsibility as they are called today at IITB - these told me I had a future in things that didn't need engineering. So I went from being General Secretary of H10 to running Mood Indigo in 1990, spending nights out at the Student Activity Centre. I think I won the Hostel GSec election on the issue of 'should we allow men into our hostel', most of us clearly wanted it and I feel a little sad that times have regressed from our self-governing days.

Mood I 1990 had a princely budget of Rs 3.5 lakh and going pitching to corporates was one of the things I did – I remember guarding a cheque of Rs 35,000 as if my life depended on it, as I travelled back from Unilever House to IITB. Managed an all-male Mood I crew and oversaw competitions, hospitality, PR and logistics-it laid the foundation for managing male-only sales teams as I started my career.

Professional Journey

I went to IIM Bangalore after IITB and here acads came a lot easier. We were the children of India's liberalization - opportunities presented themselves and I kept grabbing them. I spent more than two decades with corporate India working my way up the proverbial ladder – with companies like Titan, Unilever, Vodafone, Britannia. Worked on iconic brands and built a few new ones – my last role in Corporate was as Chief Marketing Officer for Britannia. I don't remember a day where I had to drag myself to work – for me work and fun are intertwined, can't do one without the other.

I knew I wanted a second career – wasn't sure whether it was in academia or non-profit or running a chai ki dukaan. I chose to go back to school – went to Singapore Management University for my PhD. While I was finishing my dissertation thesis, IIT Bombay reached out to come teach practitioner insights to aspiring entrepreneurs. You would think that I have been very fortunate with op-

Celebration pic with team members at Britannia

portunities – well, that is true, but I believe we make our own luck. IITB knew me as an active alum long before the faculty role came about.

I teach the 'Introduction to Entrepreneurship' elective with undergrad and post-grad students all bubbling with ideas. I go to work everyday, hoping to make a difference, to at least some project teams who are solving a relevant problem of today. 'A startup is what I want to do, and I don't see why I should do anything else' seems to be the motto. It's exciting to be a part of this revolution!

RAPID FIRE

I believe: In living life queen size
If I could, I would: Make every young person believe in themselves more than they do.
I love: Conversations.
The world needs: Tolerance and kindness
Success is: Moving ahead, upwards, and onwards. And having fun while doing so.
The most important thing to remember when I step into work: The two people I will make a difference to, today.

Giving Back to IIT

I am an out and out extrovert (I wasn't born this way), happiest meeting people, solving problems and volunteering for causes and IIT is my favourite cause. So, during our Silver Jubilee reunion I got actively involved with fundraising for legacy projects – student scholarships, entrepreneurship programs, clean energy — projects we continue to work on. We were the first $1 million batch.

Have been privileged to be able to give back to IITB through fundraising, through personally championing projects like student housing, gender issues, innovation and entrepreneurship etc. I look forward to the next decade of giving back – as an alum and as faculty member.

Challenges as a Woman

I don't remember any insurmountable challenge as a woman professional. Of course, the numbers are stacked against you and everything you do catches attention, wanted or otherwise. I started my career in Sales and travelled almost 12 days a month to small towns – many hotel rooms scared me, there weren't mobile phones then, I learned to barricade the door with a table and chairs.

I was often a lone woman in senior management meetings, and I learnt quickly that not speaking up is never an option. Women professionals have gone through the constant debate between 'blending in' and 'standing out' – you discover what works best for you. For me, it's Authenticity – I am the same person at work and otherwise, no work persona or home persona.

Work-Life Balance

I don't want to use platitudes like my husband supports me – that would be such an understatement. Ashish is my biggest cheerleader and true to his name, a big blessing in my life. We met at IIM Bangalore and our sales careers took us to different extremities of the country – Ahmedabad and Guwahati, Delhi and Cochin – and our friends joked that we would meet at Nagpur railway station to say our wedding vows and leave immediately to sell watches and paints.

My idea of work-life balance is not reducing work or life but maximizing both! It comes with some stresses, but I don't remember missing any school function or work or a family or social function for that matter.

We have a son, Adi, who was brought up by grandparents, friends and neighbours, nannies and housekeepers, I used to call our community a kibbutz lifestyle with other kids and their parents becoming one large supportive family. Every evening, I would tell Adi about what happened with me at work, and he would tell me what happened at school. Today, thanks to messaging and video calls, these rituals continue and I get to see Adi's friends and the support system he has built for himself in California.

Advice to Young Women

Grab every opportunity. Learn to recognize opportunities, they come masked at times. Reach out and network, you never know what each connection will get you. Focus not just on academics but on overall personality and roundedness.

AWARDS & HONORS

- Economic Times Power Puff Girls, Women Professionals to watch for, 2004.
- Marketing & Advertising – Cannes 2002, Effies 2012 & 2014, DMAI Digital Award 2012.
- Rated #18 in Impact Most Influential Women in Media, Marketing, Advertising, 2014.
- Distinguished Service Alumni Award, IIT Bombay 2016.

Alaska cruise with family: younger daughter Anjali on left, older daughter Shalini on right and husband Arun Majumdar

All women should be financially independent."

FLUID DYNAMIC

I started as a software engineer, but realized I want to be on the business side.

Early Life

I grew up in a small town called Bhilai. My dad worked as an engineer in the steel plant and in our colony almost everyone's father was an engineer. My dad's two brothers were engineers. So was my cousin, she was in fact the first female engineer hired by Bhilai steel plant. A very inspiring person for me as well.

Dad was quite busy and stressed at work so it was my mom who taught us maths and physics at home. She was a math teacher at English Middle School in Sector 10. I always excelled in Math and Physics and also saw my brother studying for the JEE so I was inspired by him to try for it myself.

During our time, there was only 1 entrance exam as opposed to now where there is a screening exam as well as the actual one. Also, they would only take about top 1000 students into any of the IITs. So I knew it would be hard but I studied diligently and made the cut.

My older brother went to IIT Kanpur but I chose to join IIT Bombay. It was for a very practical reason - there was a direct train from Bombay to Bhilai. Another reason was my parents thought there is a high probability that I might meet a Maharashtrian guy. Well, I did meet someone in IIT Bombay and we did get married but he is not a Maharashtrian.

Life at IIT Bombay

On reaching campus I found out that I was the first girl after 10 years in Mechanical Engineering. That did not deter me and I really enjoyed my courses.

The guys at that time used to be very shy. If one guy had the courage to talk to us, then the other guys would tease him. So it was a very lonely ex-

DR. ARUNA JOSHI

B.Tech, Mechanical Engineering, 1985

Vice President, Model Risk Management at Visa

Adjunct faculty at the University of San Francisco

SCUBA diving in Japan with daughters

> "IIT BOMBAY, TO ME IS: MY STEPPING STONE. I WOULDN'T BE WHERE I AM WITHOUT IIT BOMBAY.

perience. Going to class and getting help in understanding the material was a challenge. But other aspects more than made up for it.

In the hostel we had a lot of fun. There were few women in undergrad (only 4 in a class of about 200). But there were a lot of women in the masters program. We had Mood Indigo, inter-hostel competitions and cultural programs. All extremely fond memories for me. I used to sing and also participate in sports. In fact, I represented IIT Bombay in badminton.

One professor in IIT who really inspired me was Professor Sukhatme. The passion with which he taught was incredible. I understood everything. And that's how I decided to go

into heat transfer and fluid mechanics. After my Master's from Iowa State University. I did a PhD in computational fluid dynamics and heat transfer from UC Berkeley.

Professional Journey

It was at UC Berkeley that I met my husband Arun Majumdar. Actually, we were both classmates in Mechanical Engineering in IIT but I barely knew him then. At Berkeley, we were both graduate students, we started dating and eventually got married.

Initially, I really wanted to be a professor of engineering. But at that time, universities had a rule that they would not hire husband and wife in the same department. So I decided to work in industry as a mechanical engineer. I worked at an environmental consulting company while my husband was a professor at UC Santa Barbara.

Then my husband got an opportunity to move to Berkeley and that's how I ended up in software in the financial field. My employer didn't care that I knew nothing about finance. They were just happy that I knew Fortran. But over time I realised that what I

31st wedding anniversary with husband, Arun Majumdar in Bora Bora, French Polynesia

really wanted was to be on the business side rather than just code based on specs.

So I decided to get yet another degree - a Master's in Financial Engineering from UC Berkeley - and started working in an insurance company related to mortgages. After that, I switched to banking and worked at Union Bank, Wells Fargo and Bank of the West until Visa approached me to head their brand new department for model risk management.

RAPID FIRE

I believe: There is a lot of untapped potential within women.
I love: Pushing myself to be extreme.
The world needs: More compassion and empathy.
I'm passionate about: Sustainability, I believe in reduce, reuse, recycle.
The stuff I don't sweat: Things that are beyond my control.
Success is: How happy you are in life. **The most important thing to remember When I step into work:** Have I achieved something today?

Model Risk Management

So what is model risk management. Well, let's say you want to apply for a credit card. So what the bank does is look at your social security numbers and run a model behind the scenes based on certain information you provide. The model calculates a score and recommends whether to give you a credit card or not. And if yes, what kind of limit.

After the financial crisis of 2008, regulators came down hard on the banks saying that banks were using models but nobody was looking at what the models were doing, how exactly the calculations are being carried out and if they were accurate.

They recommended setting up an independent group within the bank to do a thorough review and manage the lifecycle of the model from initiation until retirement. This is called 'model risk management'.

So what my department does is scrutinise every single model that is being used at Visa. It has to be validated by our group. Funnily enough, the most challenging thing about this role is not technical or mathematical but just to get a buy-in from the folks in the company who build these models.

Work-Life Balance

I have two daughters and it was a bit of a challenge bringing them up because I was working full time throughout their childhood. Luckily, I had a lot of support from my parents, as well as my mother-in-law. I would say six to eight months in a year, we had either my mother-in-law or my parents staying with us.

However I decided to take it a little bit easy with jobs that had a good work-life balance when they were young. I wanted to attend every single game they had, every swim meet, drive them around, piano recitals and everything. I also wanted to make sure that my career did not take a backseat, especially after they were on their own.

So I attended a lot of evening classes just to keep up my skills. I took courses in C, C ++, Java, a lot of programming related classes, because the only exposure I had in college was Fortran. My philosophy in life is to go with the flow and to make the most of everything I have. I have no regrets.

Incidentally, both my daughters also became engineers. My older daughter, Shalini went to Caltech, worked at Microsoft for five years and right now she's finishing her MBA from Wharton. My younger daughter, Anjali got her engineering degree from Stanford and she's working at Rivian, an electric pickup truck company.

Challenges as a Woman

Just like in IIT, I am always in minority at work since the representation of women in not only engineering but also in finance is quite low. I did not have many female role models and so I always consulted my husband for any career related matters. He is very successful himself but has been a pillar for me. He is a great mentor.

Advice to Young Women

All women should be financially independent. And a STEM degree is a fantastic way as that is almost a guarantee that they'll never be unemployed. There will be challenges along the way. But if you're really focused and really passionate about what you're doing, you can cope up.

Family picture with my parents

POSITIVE VIBES

I have taken many risks in my career and ventured on roads less travelled.

Early Life

I grew up in Delhi, in the railway colony. One of my fondest memories is holding my father's hand and watching the Railway Band play music at the spring carnival every year. When I was very little, I actually wanted to be a bandmaster! Later, of course, my love and aptitude for the sciences drew me to engineering. Seeing many of the smart kids in the colony go to IIT, I decided to give it a shot.

My father was from Gujarat and my mother from Rajasthan. I enjoyed rich cultural traditions from both sides and my summer holidays were spent with cousins. At home, there was a focus on building a solid work ethic and finding my own way. My dad was the guiding light and my mother, a loving presence. We had to be disciplined and follow rules - be home by seven and sit down to study. In hindsight, all the hard work really paid off.

I was fortunate enough to clear JEE but at my rank, I was offered material science, a super interesting field but I didn't know much about it. I joined IIT Bombay thinking I would give myself a month, to see if I wanted to study material science. At the end of two weeks, my father came to visit. By then, I was in love with the place, and could not imagine studying anywhere else.

Life at IIT Bombay

The first year was challenging as it was a common curriculum for the entire batch and there was relative grading. Your grade was dependent on the grade of the smartest person in the class. There was a lot of levelling up as I came from a different board and hadn't studied some curriculum topics in my 12th grade. Coming to terms with the reality of being around people much smarter

DAMINI KUMARI

B. Tech, Materials Science Engineering, 1991

Leadership, Performance and Life Coach, Mindfulness Trainer

"Success is not winning a race, it is scripting and living a beautiful life."

than me was challenging. At the time, it felt overwhelming, but down the line, those grades don't really matter much. There is so much more to success.

A lot of things we had to put up with would be unacceptable behavior to-day. There was catcalling, ragging, judging and objectification. To be 15 girls in a batch of 300 put us under the spotlight. Thank God I had a good group of girlfriends - we supported each other through it all. I have to add there were loads of friendly and helpful boys as well, who helped normalize things and included us in fun activities on campus.

On the positive side, we had many opportunities. All we had to do was say yes! Be it on the basketball court, sports track, or the drama club. There was a perennial shortage of girls, so all were welcome. Almost the entire girls contingent played basketball to make up the girls team, no matter the ability. I was a badminton player and there was this one time when my wingmate Maneesha and I beat the

In the end, It is a solo journey... one with nature

boys on the badminton court. It created so much hungama!

And of course, IITB is where I met my life partner, Rajeev. We met on the badminton court and had so much fun being part of the IIT Bombay badminton team. We would study together, hang out with friends and go out late night to the campus canteen. He's the one who got me through one of my toughest subjects – Physics 2.

"

IIT BOMBAY, TO ME IS: THE MOST PRECIOUS FOUR YEARS OF MY LIFE.

Professional Journey

I went to IIM Lucknow after my B.Tech. and started my career in finance at ICICI Securities in their equity research division. I covered commodities and visited steel plants and aluminium factories. I remember writing a report on Hindalco when they went for their ADR offering. I learned a lot and enjoyed every moment of it.

IIT... Woh bhi kya din the!

Rajeev's work gave us the opportunity to live in different parts of the world. I reinvented myself wherever I went. In UK, I became a research fellow at Aberdeen Business School. In the year 2000, we returned to India at a time when business television was taking off.

CNBC TV18 was looking to hire a markets anchor – someone to report on the stock markets for television and I was keen on the job. Their CEO, Haresh Chawla, also from IIT Bombay, interviewed me and I joined CNBC as Associate Editor. I went into the deep end of business television, learning all about crisp, incisive communication and story telling. I was the only anchor with no prior journalism experience but I learned fast. I had to.

It was an exciting time, covering live markets for prime time business TV, interviewing the top brass of corporate India, creating innovative programming content. A few years later, in 2012, I attended a self-development program which made me reflect on intentional living and explore my true passion and area of contribution. I realised that I was coasting along but I was certainly not the best version of myself. I wanted more. And that's how my journey into coaching began.

Reinventing Myself

I'm obsessed with the question of how people thrive. Martin Seligman's PERMA model posits five areas as critical for happiness: positive emotions, engagement, relationships, meaning and achievement. My focus is to address the knowing-doing gap in these five areas. I use principles of psychology, neuroscience and mindfulness practice to help people bridge that gap.

I worked to get my certification in coaching. It was a humbling experi-

Dad... honest critic and most ardent supporter

IIT gave me the love for mountaineering

RAPID FIRE

I believe: Life plays out like a game of bridge. We can't control the hand dealt to us but we most certainly can play it to the best of our ability. Therein lies the magic… in the game play… not the final outcome

If I could, I would: Build a world without borders, no passports, no visas.

I love: The tenacity of life.

I'm passionate about: The mysteries of the mind.

I wish: To see what's on the other side of the veil of death. I have lost loved ones and I want answers.

ence to once again be a newcomer in a field and start by clocking coaching hours. A coach helps you learn about yourself, your personality, strengths and weaknesses, and relationships. A coach partners with clients to help them achieve their dreams and aspirations.

A coach helps script and create success. What may feel like a stellar achievement to one person may feel like abject failure to another. Hence setting realistic expectations that generates the right kind of energy is a big part in the game.

For me, success is not winning a race. Rather it is scripting and living a beautiful life. It revolves around the idea of making the most of life's opportunities whilst holding one's limitations and shortcomings with tenderness. It requires our experiencing self, one that lives and breathes experiences, and our evaluating self, one that judges experiences as good or bad, to work together in tandem.

Work-Life Balance

I have taken many risks in my career and ventured on roads less travelled. This allowed me to explore new fields, learn new skills and embrace interesting opportunities. Most importantly, it allowed me to take time out to spend with my children when they were little.

We lived in 6 countries over the last 25 years and I have ensured the kids never came back to an empty home. The years in television were very hectic and I was fortunate to have help from both our parents – they would fill in when I had to be away.

I have been extremely fortunate to have a supportive family that has always encouraged me to pursue my career. My kids are now grown up and working. They push me to set challenging goals for myself. Life has come full circle!

Advice to Young women

As a young girl, I remember being hypersensitive and emotionally vulnerable. I would get very upset if I didn't meet my expectations. I was easily overwhelmed and stressed. Luckily, I had the good sense to reach out for support – be it from family or friends, It made all the difference. Talking about your problems not only helps find solutions but also helps build deeper friendships. Lean in!

One off the bucket list...
Everest Base Camp

"Feminism means... that men and women have the same opportunity to live out their dreams".

THE ACCIDENTAL BIOLOGIST

I started as a software engineer, but realized I want to be on the business side.

Early Life

I remember when I was young, people would say, "Oh, you are Geeta Narlikar? So pleased to meet you". And my younger sister, Girija, and I would wonder, "Are you pleased to meet us because of who we are? Or because of our last name?" Actually, only when we went outside the TIFR campus did we have any inkling of how famous our dad is.

Inside the house, it was like a normal family. My dad - astrophysicist Dr Jayant Narlikar - is a really humble person. My mom, Mangala Narlikar, is a mathematician and so was my grandfather, Vishnu Narlikar. The culture in our home shaped how I view science and the place of women in it. For their times, my parents were very progressive. There was nothing a girl 'could not do'.

My first love was physics, so I appeared for the JEE exam, hoping to do Engineering Physics. Unfortunately, my rank was too low. I was told that if I want to do basic science at IIT, chemistry is the only other option. To my surprise, I started enjoying chemistry and stuck with it. I learnt that sometimes when you don't get what you want and choose something different, it can open up new paths.

Life at IIT Bombay

Apart from academics, what was really special about IIT was the close set of friendships with the women - there were just 15 of us in a class of about 300. It was a privilege to be amongst so many brilliant young

DR. GEETA NARLIKAR

M.Sc., Chemistry, 1992

Professor of Biochemistry & Biophysics
Lewis and Ruth Cozen Chair,
University of California,
San Francisco

Family photo taken in 1984. From left, Jayant (dad), Geeta, Mangala (mom) carrying Leelavati (youngest sister) and Girija (middle sister)

> **IIT BOMBAY, TO ME IS: A VERY IMPORTANT, VERY FORMATIVE TIME OF MY LIFE.**

women who have gone on to have leading careers in diverse fields.
I remember going down to the mess, having chai, having tiffin, wondering what was for tiffin and whether we would like it or not. Small joys and pleasures. At IIT, I was introduced to mountaineering, running and also to my life partner, Alok Srivastava. His love for wildlife and nature also helped me see the wonders of biology.

Prof. Durani and Prof. K.K.Rao helped me see that I could use my chemistry training to ask questions in biology. When looking at PhD programs, I chose a group at Stanford which was using chemical principles to study biological questions. That's how my journey, my transition into biology started. And I am still striving to be a biologist to be honest.

Professional Journey

I carried out postdoctoral research on chromatin remodelling enzymes at the Massachusetts General Hospital with Robert Kingston. Since 2003, I have been a faculty member in the Department of Biochemistry and Biophysics at the University of California, San Francisco where I lead a research lab.
We are told in textbooks that our

genetic material, DNA, codes for life. My lab, is trying to uncover the mysteries of how the same genetic material allows for so many different types of cells in a human being. For example, heart cells and lung cells have the same genetic material, yet they look and behave very differently. Why is that?

We are getting at these questions by studying how the genetic material is packaged in cells and how differences in the packaging can explain different cell behaviors. Our studies involve discovering the inner workings of biological molecules that do the job of packaging DNA. You could say that we 'interrogate' these biological molecules in test tubes to get at their secrets.

And in doing so with the students and postdoctoral fellows in my group, we often go into new, uncharted territory. When that happens, we ask ourselves, can we shine a light onto new areas of biology? Can we uncover new fundamental principles to understand how genes are regulated? Or, how gene regulation goes 'bad' and how you can get diseases like cancer?

We are addressing such questions from an interdisciplinary perspective, which makes the process all the more fun. When we start out on a project, we think we have a certain set of questions. But as we discover more behaviors of these biological molecules or systems, new questions emerge.

Currently, an exciting new opportunity in our field is to understand how the three-dimensional organization of the genome and the associated material and chemical properties control cellular physiology. To look at such problems from different perspectives and up-level the creative process, and more importantly for basic reasons of equity, we need to make science a welcoming place for participants from historically underrepresented backgrounds.

Work-Life Balance

I feel really lucky to have Alok as my life partner. One often hears about how partners share household responsibilities 50-50. Alok has instead invented a new way of describing a partnership of equals. He compares our marriage to a tennis doubles game, where it's not 50-50. It's 75-75.

Photo of family in 2017. From left, Geeta, Kalpana (daughter) and Alok (husband)

Photo with lab members, taken in 2021

There are two people on the court, the person in the back can sometimes come in the front, and vice-versa. So each person is doing 75% rather than each person doing 50%. This way, you are always available to cover for each other. And this partnership has enabled me to do all the things that my male colleagues have been able to do.

I wasn't held back because of my partnership. My partnership actually strengthened my career.

My daughter, Kalpana, was born when I was a young faculty member and before I had tenure. Because of Alok and support from my parents and my in-laws, I was able to effectively manage the tug of war between being with Kalpana and mentoring my students.

Feminism, to me, means that men and women have the same opportunity to have an impact in the world

RAPID FIRE

I believe: There is good in everybody.
If I could, I would: Reverse climate change.
I love: Puns, PJs.
The world needs: More women in leadership and more caring people in leadership.
I'm passionate about: Having fun doing science.
Success is: Pushing yourself to take on new challenges.

and the same opportunity to live out their dreams. However whether or not this can happen depends on society. Today, in my lab there are researchers with kids and the whole team supports them when they have childcare needs - they are doing fabulously, being at their creative best. But how often do we see this in companies?

Advice to Young Women

The message I got in the beginning was you have to be 'more like a guy'. Over time, I realized that I had to invent new ways of finding success. For example, I am an introvert who felt shy to ask questions in public. So I would find the speaker after the seminar and talk to him or her one-on-one. Be authentic, you don't have to do things which make you uncomfortable in order to succeed.

I have to admit, sometimes things get crazy because every profession has politics. What helps me then is to say, these are humans, they're like molecules at some level. And when I know them over many years, I should be able to predict how they will react. This saves me disillusionment and frustration. It lets me find the good in people while being fully aware of their limitations.

What I have also learnt is that while tackling such 'people issues', I can get perspective by focusing on why I'm here in the first place, which is to enjoy doing frontier science.

AWARDS & HONORS

- Beckman Young Investigator Award (2006).
- The Leukemia and Lymphoma Society Scholar award (2008).
- The Outstanding Faculty Mentorship Award by the UCSF Graduate Students Association (2011).
- The Deleage Prize awarded by the Deleage foundation (2017).
- The Glenn Award for Research in Biological Mechanisms of Aging (2018).
- Distinguished alumni awardee, IIT Bombay (2018).
- Elected fellow of the National Academy of Sciences USA (2021).

THE TRANSFORMER

What I'm really excited and passionate about is making a valuable difference.

Early Life

A Tamilian born in Nagpur, I consider myself to be a naturalized Maharashtrian. Since my father worked in the insurance sector, I grew up in different parts of the country. But I came back to Kendriya Vidyalaya Nagpur to complete my matric (class 11). I was not the class topper but definitely in the top 5% of my class and also a National Science Talent scholar.

Education is highly valued in our family. I spent the first 3-4 years of my life with my nani, while my mother pursued a PhD in Botany from BHU. My eldest mama is from IIT KGP, the youngest from IIT Madras. My maasis hold master's degrees in physics and chemistry. Even before I could think about it, the family had decided I should go to IIT.

I must have been in grade six so the planning was that long term. An aunt would sit with me, set me challenging questions in algebra or geometry. So it was a natural kind of environment for me. I didn't take any formal coaching for JEE - it did not exist and for every subject I had a personal tutor within the family.

I am the eldest of four daughters. All my siblings have had traditional educational paths spanning accounting, software engineering and management education. I was a contrarian from a very young age, with what was considered an unacceptable, outspoken and radical worldview for a girl to have. It made my parents, especially my mother, very concerned and fairly anxious.

Life at IIT Bombay

I entered IIT as a 16-year-old and five years later, I had grown not just academically but as a person. My initial challenge was coming from a small town to the big city, the first experience of being away from home. So it

GIRIJA SUDHAKAR RAM

Masters, Dual Degree, Chemistry, 1980

Executive Director at Newgen DigitalWorks
Founders' and Promoters' Group Member, Mastek
Trustee/Director, Bhavitha Foundation

With Sudhakar at the world's oldest cast iron bridge on River Severn, Shropshire, UK

took a couple of semesters adjusting to being independent, taking my own decisions. Also, coping up with some subjects like physics (my Achilles heel).

We were just 40 girls in H10 between undergrad and post-grad, so we became really close. My hostel mates were my stress busters. They brought perspective to a bad grade or not being able to solve an open book exam. My fondest memories are simple ones like taking a walk around the

Celebrating my 35th birthday and the imminent arrival of our baby

Travelling with baby Samvitha and nanny on an official trip

campus. Sitting in the H10 lounge watching Chhayageet once a week.

I discovered a whole new world, thanks to my peers. There were conversations about nihilism and existentialism - words I didn't even know existed. Very abstract thinking and philosophical questions which changed my world view. To many of my peers, everything seemed to come effortlessly while I had to struggle. But I think that builds character and keeps you grounded.

Over time, I realised that I am not meant for a STEM career. I could not see myself in fundamental research or R&D or as an academic. By a process of elimination I decided that if I want to break out, my best bet is to do an MBA. I joined IIM Calcutta and discovered the importance of EQ. And that part, which had never been nourished in IIT came to flower.

"

IIT BOMBAY, TO ME IS: A GORGEOUS PLACE THAT TRANSFORMED ME FROM A CATERPILLAR TO A BUTTERFLY.

Professional Journey

I entered the world of sales and marketing and had a very satisfying stint with Cadbury's where I became a marketing manager. I was married to my IIMC batchmate Sudhakar Ram, we were happy as DINKs (Double Income No Kids). Sudhakar was working with Rediffusion advertising as CTO but in 1984, he joined a startup called Mastek as a co-founder.

At that time Mastek had a 100 sq ft office in Nariman Point which did not even have 4 chairs. But Sudhakar was from a family business background and was clear that he didn't want to work for anyone else. So I became the main breadwinner of the family while he struggled for over a decade to grow Mastek to a point where there was stable cash flow.

After a decade, I moved to Raymond where I had the profit center responsibility and a mandate to transform the apparel business. I remember, during the interview, Vijaypat Singhania asked me a question, "Madam, what do you know about textiles?" I said, "Sir, if that is the reason you're hiring me, we shouldn't even be talking. Apparel is not about fabric, it's about lifestyle."

I got hired and was, in fact, the only woman in the general management team at the time. I understood the strength of Raymond (distribution network) and also the problem (branding). Over the next 6 years, we made Park Avenue, the largest menswear brand in the country. And then my daughter was born and everything changed.

Managing Motherhood

We were both completely absorbed in our careers, the kind who never watched the clock. I had a baby in my mid-30s, after 13 years of marriage, which was unheard of back then. Motherhood was a completely transformative experience. From a crazy uni-focussed career woman, I became multidimensional. I no longer wanted to work endless hours or live out of a suitcase.

Four months post-Samvitha's birth, I said to Sudhakar, "I want to resign". He was my biggest cheerleader, he knew work would keep me energized and make me a positive influence on my daughter. So he said, "Girija, you forget that I have a 50% stake in this venture. Now can you please go to work? I will take care of Samvitha."

And he truly kept that promise. Sudhakar used to take my little baby to the office (he was CEO of Mastek) while I travelled for work. The understanding was that I would give myself 3 years in corporate life and if I still didn't like it, I could quit. For those three years, he was more of a parent to my daughter than I was. He cooked and read for her, sang her to sleep, kept an eye on her during meetings.

In 1999, I quit Raymond to become my own boss. One of my assignments was as a consultant to Madura Garments. I was attracted by the intellectual challenge of integrating the textiles business with the apparel business that Aditya Birla group had acquired. Side by side, I became a co-promoter with my brother-in-law, in what we now call a startup.

Taking the Plunge

It was sort of fortuitous that my brother-in-law graduated from college and wanted to start a digital publishing business. He was in his mid-20s, I was in my mid-30s, so it was a chance to put my skills to the test. What I am passionate about is growth and transformation. Give me something which is already running smoothly - that's not my forte.

NewGen's customers were large publishers in law and STEM. The challenge was to make the company cash rich and strategically move up the value chain. From typesetting to copy editing to project management to digitization, the whole process took 5 years.

This arrangement also allowed me to be master of my own destiny, and my

Fulfilling a 23 year old vow- Samvitha's wedding at Tirupati

time. Today work from home is common but it was not so in the 90s. We lived in a duplex, so I had my office on the first floor. Later, when Sudhakar relocated to the UK and US, I continued working remotely. My daughter grew up with global influences, imbibing our conversations, our love for books.

RAPID FIRE

I believe: I can.
If I could, I would: Travel the length and breadth of India, the real India.
I love: Classical music and dancing, my daughter and happy children.
The world needs: More compassionate and empathetic people.
The stuff I don't sweat: What the world thinks of me.
Success is: Making a difference to someone's life.

Change is a Constant

When we returned to India after Sudhakar's global stint he became captivated with Mahatma Gandhi. We travelled extensively across his janambhoomi - Tamil Nadu - and his karambhoomi Maharashtra. We visited many NGOs doing ground-level work. It was a huge learning experience as we had set up Bhavitha Foundation, to work on various social causes.

On November 8, 2020, Sudhakar passed away after battling cancer. He remained his positive self right

till the end, attending the AGM of Mastek two weeks before he passed away. No one knew he was critically ill. During his lifetime I had no involvement with Mastek but now I see it as his legacy and hence, am part of the Founders' Group. I also interact regularly with the Executive Leadership Team.

Sudhakar's biggest legacy of course is Samvitha, who is all of 27 now. She went to Princeton, where she graduated magna cum laude and works with McKinsey in New York. I divide my time between Newgen, Mastek, Bhavitha and educating my maid's four kids, who are my foster children. The oldest, Gayatri, is 15 while the youngest, Vighnesh, is just 5 years old. I care deeply about the kids and transforming their future. I am actively involved in their education and upbringing - I interact regularly with their teachers and school administrators.

Seeing these children blossom gives me immense joy. I have many thoughts on how we can transform K-12 education in India. I hope I get an opportunity to do that someday.

-

Challenges as a Woman

Regardless of my IIT-IIM degree, I had to work twice as hard to be treated at par with my male counterparts. I created history by moving to a sales role in Cadburys. The distributors and sales managers were all male, it was their first ever experience of interacting with an assertive woman professional. At Raymond, I was the only woman at the General Management Level. One had to be exceptionally resilient to deal with the unstated patriarchal system.

Advice to Young Women

If you have natural aptitude for math and sciences, go for a STEM education. It will give you a solid foundation in certain critical thinking skills that will stand you in good stead.

AWARDS & HONORS

- Gold Medallist, IIT Bombay (1976)
- Distinguished Alumna Awardee, IIT Bombay (2005)
- Small Business Innovation Research Award, US Air Force

"You are capable of a lot more than you imagine!"

With my parents (Ananthy and Krishna Kalpathy) and son (Avilash Cramer) at Acadia National Park in Maine, USA

BIOMED BOSS

I work at the intersection of computer science, mathematics and medical imaging.

Early Life

I am an only child. My father was a director at E.Merck, a pharmaceutical company. I attended St. Anthony's in Chembur. I think people would say that I was a good student. I was generally quiet and shy and a bookworm.

My mother was a physics professor at SIES college in Bombay and from very early on, she made me feel that women can do anything they want. I was fortunate to be born in such a home and have a great role model in the family.

My mother was often grading papers at home or preparing for her lectures. I asked her lots of questions about science and physics. I remember learning about atoms and circuits, well before I was exposed to those concepts at school or college. So, from a young age, I was really excited excited about what opportunities there were in physics and engineering.

I prepared for JEE by studying at home by myself. I did attend one short course at Agrawal classes.

Life at IIT Bombay

I think for most of us it was the first time we were living away from home. So the hostel and campus became a new home, new family in a sense. In terms of activities, I was introduced to rock climbing in IIT due to 'Himankan', the mountaineering club. That developed into a lifelong love of climbing. I also participated in inter-IIT (badminton).

We were 11 girls in a batch of roughly 300, so you could say the gender ratio was quite unbalanced! Regardless

DR. JAYSHREE KALPATHY-CRAMER

B.Tech, Electrical engineering, 1987

Chief, Division of Artificial Medical Intelligence, Department of Ophthalmology, University of Colorado Anschutz Medical Campus

Associate Professor of Radiology at the Massachusetts General Hospital, Harvard Medical School

Himankan 84, a student led trip by the IITB mountaineering club, introduced me to the outdoors. Though the trip was physically challenging for me, I developed a lifelong appreciation of mountains and nature.

With Dr. S. Arunkumar at IITB

of that, we had to get used to working a lot harder than ever before. And it was very challenging, very rigorous work but you got the hang of it. In terms of the education itself, IIT was fabulous. It gave me a very strong foundation which allowed you to do whatever you want in life, not just the field you actually studied. Prof. Vasi was a phenomenal mentor. Due to his influence, I not only developed an interest in semiconductors but I got exposed to the world of books and literature.

Professional Journey

I did my PhD at the Rensselaer Polytechnic Institute in Troy, NY and that's also where I met my husband. He was working on his mathematics PhD when we met.

After working in the semiconductor industry for a decade and a half, I pivoted to a career in health informatics and radiology. In fact, in 2010, I went back to school and did a Master's in Biomedical Informatics through Oregon Health and Science University.

It was a multidisciplinary program with a very international cohort which included clinicians, doctors and computer scientists. All my life, I've been in the data analysis field in

"

IIT BOMBAY, TO ME IS: THE PLACE WHERE I GREW UP, BECAME A GOOD ENGINEER.

some way. My background from IIT and core engineering principles have been really helpful both in semiconductors and in healthcare.

The work that we do is the application of machine learning and AI for a variety of health care applications, specifically in medical imaging. We have a lot of existing data from patients. Are there patterns in this data that can be used to treat patients in the future, to improve health care, to reduce the cost, to make it more efficient?

In short, our goal is to develop algorithms that might be useful for diagnosis and treatment-It's a real intersection of computer science, mathematics and medical imaging.

Making a Difference

The work we've done in ophthalmology and oncology has the potential to be truly impactful. We work in a disease called retinopathy of prematurity (ROP), which is a condition of premature or low birth weight babies. Due to advances in health care, such babies have a much higher rate of survival. But if they're in a neonatal ICU and not managed properly, they can develop blindness.

ROP can be treated but needs to be diagnosed early. So we've developed an algorithm that can be used in remote settings in conjunction with clinicians, so that they can identify the population that needs to be screened the most. We are hoping that this algorithm will get deployed worldwide, including India.

The other problem we are working on is screening for cervical cancer using low-cost approaches in low-resource settings. Again, we are partnering with leading experts to develop algorithms that can be used in large screening programs where AI can help improve the consistency and the diagnostic process. Hopefully, what is a fairly qualitative process becomes much more quantitative.

I find my work to be both exciting and satisfying! Recently, I was selected to lead the new Artificial Medical Intelligence Division at the CU Department of Ophthalmology.

With my father (Krishna Kalpathy) at IIT on convocation day (1987)

Challenges as a Woman

I think that there were definitely some challenges of being in a minority at IIT. But most of the engineering conferences that I go to today are hardly different. I mean, there are very, very few women. I think that life at IIT prepared me well and allowed me to be comfortable in situa-

Climbing in Joshua Tree National Park, 2019

RAPID FIRE

I believe: Climate change is a serious threat that will have very unequal impacts across the globe. We should be acting more aggressively to combat its worst effects.

If I could, I would: Enjoy the outdoors more

I love: my family, I love my students, I love the mountains, I love climbing.

The world needs: A lot more women in positions of leadership.

If you fall: Dust up, get up, proudly show your scars.

The stuff I don't sweat: Petty politics

Success is: Doing something that improves the lives of others.

tions where I am the only woman at the table.

That's a tricky one and there's no one right answer. I was pregnant during the last part of my PhD and I hoped to finish before my son was born. But he came a little early. So what should have taken a month to finish took six months. And then I took a couple years off because it was important to me that I spent time with him.

I have had a lot of family support throughout my life. My husband has always been very involved - he does a lot of work around the house, is a phenomenal cook and a great father. I was often travelling for work so he was the one who went to the parent-teacher meetings when my son was young. My parents also helped out tremendously. We could not have managed without their help.

The first two years when I stayed home with my son were really rich and very highly rewarding years, 100% worth it. But it probably set my career back in a sense. On the other hand, we were empty nesters much earlier than our peers and I could spend a lot of time on my career later in life.

Similarly, I was working in the semiconductor industry and it was going great but I decided that it was time to try something else. And then we had this opportunity to go abroad with my husband's job and again, it was a work-life balance moment. I took the time off and reset my career. So there's definitely been sort of fits and starts to my career, but I think all of it has been helpful.

Advice to Young Women

When you think you are stuck remember, you are capable of a lot more than you imagine. Step back and reflect on what is really meaningful to you.

With my husband (Alan Cramer) and son (Avilash Cramer), 1993

THE VISIONARY

To me, students are the best part of this job, they are so energizing to be around.

Early Life

I am a Tamilian who grew up in a middle class home in Mumbai. We were a large family - my parents, brother, sister, uncle and me - living in a small apartment in Pali Hill, Bandra. My father and my uncle were initially in the Indian Air Force, and later, airline pilots with Air India. My mother was a homemaker who never got a chance to go to college.

As a child, I learnt Bharatnatyam and at some point, I thought I could go on to become a classical dancer. But I also enjoyed math and science and my older brother Krishna was a big influence in my life. He was studying Electrical Engineering at VJTI and encouraged me to think of engineering as a career. At that time, it was an unusual career path for a girl.

I studied with a group of friends at Ruparel college who were also working hard to get in. I did not think I would qualify at all, far less did I expect to get a high enough rank to qualify for computer science. I was definitely very surprised. I think my JEE rank was 131 (but not sure).

Life at IIT Bombay

The IIT experience was a culture shock. I found it intensely competitive and, as you know, that can be stressful. But, looking back, I just remember the good times, the deep friendships I formed. 30 years later, we can still pick up a conversation with each other, where we left off.

What else? Mood Indigo, walks to Powai lake, professors teaching us amazing, deep stuff in class. The computer lab - gosh, it was always freezing! - so many nights spent working there. And after an all-nighter we'd go to this unhygienic noodle place (wonder if it still exists!) or go to watch the sunrise.

DR. KAVITA BALA

B.Tech, Computer Science, 1992

\Professor, Cornell University and the Dean of the Cornell Ann Bowers College of Computing and Information Science

"You won't know
what you like, till
you try it."

Kavita Bala, Dean of the Cornell Bowers College of Computing and Informatiion Science, with students during commencement 2022

The year I was involved with Mood Indigo we were incredibly lucky to watch Naseerudin Shah in 'Waiting for Godot'. I got to see him up close, from the floor in front of the stage. It was an astounding performance. It is a tough play and was not a crowd pleaser, but his every movement (subtle or large) was so perfect, he was mesmerizing to watch. I was transfixed.

We had about 15 women in my batch, I was the only one in computer science. H10 was at one end of the campus and we had one dial-up phone in the hostel foyer. I couldn't just drop into the guys hostel in the middle of the night, which is when you work on assignments. So I had to learn to do things by myself, become self-reliant.

When I went to do my PhD at MIT, I joined a study group with two other women and I was thrilled. When they were complaining bitterly about how MIT didn't have enough women I said, look, you have it good here, there are three of us!

IIT BOMBAY, TO ME IS: WHERE I SHAPED MY THINKING, SHAPED MY VALUES.

The professors at IIT who had a big influence on me: Prof. A. A. Diwan (AAD) who was an amazing teacher and opened our eyes to knowledge and the excitement of open-ended problems in computer science. DMD (Prof. Dhamdhere) held us to high standards of excellence, I enjoyed working with him on my Bachelor's project. DBP (Prof. Phatak) was energizing.

Professional Journey

At MIT, initially I was thinking of working on compilers research. When the faculty member I was working with left, I had to look for another project. At that time, Prof.

Seth Teller and Prof. Julie Dorsey joined MIT and I was excited by the work they were doing. I switched to computer graphics and did my PhD thesis in the area of visual computing.

I came to Cornell as a post-doctoral researcher and have spent almost my entire working life here. What excites me about this area is trying to understand how human beings perceive the world, and using that knowledge to drive better graphics and vision. Digital prototyping tools, architectural visualizations, movies and games are all applications that use computer generated imagery that looks real. To produce that realism, you need to make an image that represents reality by simulating the physics, by getting shapes right, by making things look right.

For example, a recent body of work that my group has done is understanding why silk looks like silk or velvet looks like velvet. It turns out that you, a human being, can immediately differentiate silk from velvet. But for an algorithm to get that right, you need to simulate the structure of these materials, the physics of the light interacting with the material to produce the characteristic highlights and reflections that make them look the way they do.

On the computer vision side. I'vebeen fascinated by how people understand images. You look at me, you immediately recognize me. You see a cup on a table, you immediately know what it is. But for a computer algorithm to do it has been hard until recently; there's a big area of research called 'scene understanding' that studies this.

Shaping the Future

When I started in computer science, it was a purely academic discipline. What's changed now is the real world impact of the work that we are doing.

Computer Science, Class of 1992, IIT Powai with Faculty members, Prof. D.B. Phatak, Prof. A. A. Diwan and Prof. Dhamdhere

Outside the Gates Building

In 2015, I had the crazy, exciting opportunity to co-found a startup - GrokStyle - with my PhD student Sean Bell. The company was born out of visual recognition research we did together.

We decided to focus on home décor. So, you could take a picture of any piece of furniture and the AI would tell you exactly what make it is. You say, "Oh, that's great. That's exactly what I wanted" and you can potentially buy it.

When we launched, we rolled out GrokStyle's recognition capability as a part of IKEA's augmented reality app. Then in 2018, we got acquired by Facebook and now our core technology is in Facebook's visual recognition software called GrokNet. So it's being used by millions of people and that's incredibly exciting for us.

I came back to Cornell to be chair of the computer science department and then the dean of the College of Computing and Information Science, which was recently named the Cornell Bowers College of Computing and Information Science. I realized that my heart lies in academia. I want to educate the next generation.

RAPID FIRE

I believe: In the power of education.
The world needs: People learning to talk across differences.
I'm passionate about: Mentoring the next generation.
I wish: I could get a glimpse of what technologies will look like 100 years from now.
The stuff I don't sweat: Don't try to be perfect in everything.

Women in Computer Science

At Cornell, we have about 2000+ majors in computing and information science, of which 43% are women. The national average is 20%. What we find is that women and men are equally good but it's important to create the right community so that the learning environment isn't unnecessarily hostile and cutthroat. Once you do that, all students thrive. I have had the good fortune of having great mentors, and now I am a mentor for a lot of women in computer graphics. I strongly recommend that no matter what stage of life you are in, find somebody junior to you whom you can be a mentor to. Give forward. After all, we are all standing on the shoulders of those who believed in us and supported us.

My mother is from a very educated family, but for various reasons, she only finished high school. Yet she has supported me my entire life, every step of the way. When IITB conferred the Distinguished Alumnus Award, I could not travel due to Covid. I asked my mother to receive it on my behalf. For her, it was deeply meaningful to be there.

Work-Life Balance

Well, it is a tightrope. My husband, Andrew Myers, is also a professor at Cornell and we decided early on that having children was important for us. In fact, we knew that we wanted to have three children. And we couldn't wait till both of us had tenure, we felt like we had to live our life now and balance having kids with our careers.

I had my first child as a postdoctoral researcher which was really tough. Luckily by then, Andrew was a tenure track professor. When we had our second child, we were both tenure track professors. So juggling two careers, two kids and everything related to kids like falling sick, picking them up, dropping them off, all that stuff, was challenging.

One thing we did to keep our sanity a little bit is we spaced them out. I have a 21-year-old, a 17-year-old and a 12-year-old. Also, we had an incredibly supportive family, who helped us tremendously: my mother, my uncle, my father. I would say we lead a demanding life which is more like a kind of 'managed chaos'.

Typically, I get up at 4 am and between 4-8 am is when I can get a lot of concentrated work done. At about 8 am, my meetings start and go on until about 6 pm.

Advice to Young Women

First, you won't know what you like till you try it. And second, I really think we are in a very fortunate time. You can try different things. You can take risks. If you do a start-up, it could succeed. It could fail. That's fine. If it doesn't work out, it's not life or death in terms of your career. You can bounce back and still find a path to success.

AWARDS & HONORS

- IIT Bombay Distinguished Alumnus Award (2021)
- SIGGRAPH Computer Graphics Achievement Award (2020)
- Fellow of the SIGGRAPH Academy (2020)
- Bala is an Association for Computing Machinery (ACM) Fellow (2019)
- Multiple Cornell teaching awards (2006, 2009, 2015)

MATH MAGIC

Mathematicians come in all stripes and colours.

Early Life

My father is a mathematician doing research in algebraic geometry while my mother worked as a librarian and translates English books into Tamil. I was privileged to have grown up in the TIFR (Tata Institute of Fundamental Research) housing colony, where I lived in a building with 99 apartments. I got an early exposure to science there.

Dr. Venkataraman and Dr. Naranan, two professors at TIFR, arranged to screen science documentaries for all the kids in the building and Venil Naranan used to run birdwatching outings. Also, my father, a gifted expositor, would often discuss math with me casually, as we ran errands together.

I also got introduced to the world of amateur theatre by Mrs. Sundari Seshadri and performed with her in a Tamil play at Shanmukhananda Hall. At school (Cathedral and John Connon High School), I enjoyed my academics and also took part in sports, choir, elocution and debating.

My parents emphasized that I should find and follow my passion. In fact, my parents left my choice of career completely up to me, providing advice or input only if I asked for it. So, although I had many interests, in the end, I was most excited by the prospect of research in scientific fields. As my dad took a year's sabbatical at Harvard I graduated from high school in Cambridge, MA. On returning to India, I studied for the JEE, without taking Agrawal Classes, but working out their practice sheets and reading text books.

DR. KAVITA RAMANAN

B.Tech, Chemical Engineering, 1992

Roland George Dwight Richardson Professor and Associate Chair at the Division of Applied Math at Brown University

Associate Director at ICERM, Institute of Computational and Experimental Research in Mathematics, Brown University

Kavita
Ramanan
at CMU
"Passion is what will
get you through the
rough patches..."

Kavita being congratulated by Nobel Laureate Steve Chu for becoming an AAAS Fellow

Photo Courtesy: S. Pantula

"

**IIT BOMBAY,
TO ME IS: IS A PLACE THAT GENERATES SO MANY WONDERFUL, FOND MEMORIES**

Life at IIT Bombay

It was a wonderful time of my life,where I made many wonderful friends. I enjoyed the inter-hostel events, especially lit and music. For example, getting together to give small classical music concerts with other students, like fellow IITian Madhavan, who was a violinist, and Sriganesh who was a mridangist, or singing Hindi film songs during Sur-bahar, or jamming and listening to classic rock.

I would regularly play basketball in the evenings, often the only girl there, but never made to feel so. I also had an adventurous trip to IIT Delhi for an inter-IIT meet – I remember riding on top of the train to get some fresh air and after our match, accompanying Coach Edwin to a church to attend Christmas Mass.

I went for my weekly music classes with Smt. Aruna Sairam to Wadala – it was quite a journey after a full day of classes, taking a bus, two trains and finally walking through a fish market to my teacher's home. But I always came back energized and am grateful for the mess workers and my dear friend Lalita, who made sure that a plate of dinner had been saved for me.

In terms of academics, most professors were supportive. Professor Zuvekar was particularly encouraging and acted as advisor for my B.Tech.

seminar on 'Stochastic processes in reaction engineering'. Prof.U.V. Shenoy (UVS) also imparted so much energy and passion for the subjects he taught. UVS was my B.Tech. Project (BTP) advisor.

I majored in chemical engineering, but found it was too empirical for my taste. Around the end of my third year, I realized that I really liked all the mathematical aspects, the abstraction and the theory behind everything. I didn't want to just apply a formula, I wanted to know why is this the right formula? So in my final year, I took several math electives.

Finding my Bliss

Close to graduation, I remained unsure about my career path. But I recall having a Eureka moment while in the back of a taxi with my parents, suddenly saying, "I want to do a PhD in Applied Math!" Applied Math was not a well established track in India at that time, but it seemed to combine my interests perfectly.

Then I thought, "Oh my God, I haven't done enough math!' My BTP advisor cautioned me against the switch, as he felt I could more easily succeed as a chemical engineer. I decided to take the risk anyway. At the very last minute, based on the input that I may not need a Masters to get into a PhD, I applied to Brown University, which lies in Providence, RI, and New York University, as they had excellent applied math programs.

To my surprise, I got admitted to both but chose Brown since they also promised a generous fellowship. I guess Providence struck! At Brown, everyone who was admitted in my year had done way more math than me during undergrad. I wondered, am I going to make it? Luckily, I didn't get tense, just really enjoyed myself and I did fine.

After defending my PhD in Jan 1997, I got a post-doctoral fellowship in Israel. I had always intended to become a professor, since the mission and the autonomy that academia provides appealed to me, but when I got a job offer of a permanent position from Bell Labs even before graduation, I decided to get a different perspective of research before heading to academia.

Professional Journey

At Bell Labs, I worked on several problems related to what is called large deviations, which is a theory that quantifies probabilities of rare events (for example, call drops in wireless networks, or rare mutations in genetics). In such cases, one wants to not only know or ensure that an event is rare, but also be able to characterize exactly how small that probability is and what is the most likely way in which the event would occur. Using large deviations theory, my colleague and I were able to identify a scheduling discipline that we proved would be optimal. To my own surprise, this scheduling discipline was incorporated into a switch. Seeing maths applied in a real life situation was thrilling. We also got a couple of patents to our names.

After several years at Bell Labs, I was fortunate to receive offers from a couple of universities, and I chose the Department of Mathematical Sci-

Kavita and her partner, Siddharth, during a trip to Uganda

ences at Carnegie Mellon University. After spending seven memorable years there, I returned to Brown in 2010, this time as a professor.

I work in the area of probability theory and stochastic processes. Stochastic is just a fancy name for 'random'. Probability theory is the study of uncertain phenomena. Such phenomena may be uncertain because they're inherently uncertain like quantum phenomena, or it could be that they appear uncertain because you do not have enough information to predict their outcome.

I love research and also enjoy teaching and mentoring. When I see my students solve very challenging problems,and watch them grow and become full-fledged researchers, those are my proudest moments.

Challenges as a Woman

I remember at IIT, some of the fellow students said I (and other women at IIT) were wasting a seat. Finding that a ludicrous statement, since we had earned our place at IIT in the same way as any other male student, I asked, "Why do you say that?" To which they replied, "Oh, you will go get the degree and not work." I decided that wouldn't apply to me and moved on. But I know that such comments can have an adverse affect on many women.

I've heard that IIT Bombay has started a (mandatory pass / fail, zero-credit self-study) course on gender awareness. I hope this has a positive influence on the environment. At Brown, this past semester I taught a course on "Race and Gender in the Sciences", which was created due to demand from students.

It is important to create a more welcoming atmosphere to diverse groups. I once invited a young woman PhD graduate from MIT, who had recently given birth to give a talk Brown. I found funding to enable her husband to come with her to take care of the baby. But her baby fell asleep earlier than planned, and so she gave the talk holding her sleeping baby!

Work-Life Balance

Academia makes a lot of demands on one's time, especially in the

American system, where you have to be not only a researcher, teacher and mentor, but also a manager, procure funding, etc. But I do make time to do other things. Indian classical music is one of my more serious hobbies. It nourishes my soul. I also like watching theater and films, travel and hiking.

One never completely switches off from work. Sometimes when I'm humming, or in the shower, and I'm sort of thinking about something, I get a flash of insight. What we call a 'eureka moment'. Overall, I feel like I have considerable flexibility, subject to fulfilling my teaching obligations. If I want to take a break, I can do so. Most importantly, I have a wonderful partner, who helps me maintain a good work-life balance.

Taking Math to the Masses

In January, 2016, I was invited by director Nandan Kudhyadi to be the narrator and script consultant for a documentary called 'Srinivasa Ramanujan: The Mathematician and his Legacy'. I agreed to do the project because the film was to be shown at high schools across India – and I thought it may inspire more young Indian women to pursue mathematics.

I am passionate about math outreach. I lead a group called the 'Math Co-op' with the help of students at Brown. We develop open source presentations whose slides are freely accessible to anyone who wants to use them. Due to COVID, we stopped physical presentations, but continued online meetings and video presentations.

During the pandemic, I also led an initiative called 'Mathematics sin Fronteras', which is Spanish or rather Spanglish, for 'Mathematics without Borders'. We wanted to make mathematics accessible to a large Spanish speaking population and so invited some wonderful mathematicians - all women - to give virtual bilingual extracurricular lectures. I hope to lead a similar initiative in India in the coming year.

Advice to Young Women

Find your passion, and take your time to find out what you want to do. Passion is what will get you through the rough patches in any job.

Stick by your convictions, and don't be too cautious - don't hesitate to take risks.

If you take up research, you will always be pushing yourself to the boundary of what is the unknown. So you have to learn to become comfortable with being uncomfortable.

Also, do join us in the 'march for science' to spread more rationality in the world.

AWARDS & HONOURS

- Elected to the American Academy of Arts and Sciences, 2021
- Recipient of the prestigious Vannevar Bush Faculty Fellowship in 2021
- Guggenheim Fellowship, 2020

"Don't ask for special favors".

Holidaying in Alaska

BIOMED BOSS

There were so few girls at IIT Bombay, we didn't even have a ladies hostel.

Early Life

I grew up in Mumbai and attended the Convent of Jesus and Mary, an all-girls institution. After topping the class 11 SSC board exam, I went to St Xavier's College. The principal who took my interview asked me, "Why do you want to join Xavier's? Why not Sophia?" I said, "If I go to Sophia, I get no competition". He was quite struck by my reply and took me in.

We were just 20 girls in a class of 450. But it was a pleasant experience - I had no issue interacting with boys. It was my classmates who made me fill the form for IIT. "What's IIT?" I asked. They said, "Leja, it's a very good college for engineering and you will definitely get in, you are so good in math, physics and chemistry".

Back then you had to go to the IIT campus and drop the application physically. The boys did that for me. I gave the entrance exam and got through. Looking back, I must say, I got into IIT by accident. My mother was the chief matron of Bombay Hospital. She really wanted me to be a doctor. I told her that if I get into IIT, I will do engineering. If not, I'll do medicine. So if not for IIT, I would have been a doctor today.

There was a JEE rank back then as well. In fact, all the students were called for an interview in the order of the merit list, and as they applied, the seats in the various departments and at different IITs got filled and were not available for subsequent candidates. I liked chemistry and hence thought that Chemical Engineering would suit me best. And Bombay, of course, was my home town.

LEJA HATTIANGADI

B. Tech, Chemical Engineering, 1971

Adjunct Professor, Department of Chemical Engineering, IIT Bombay

Independent Director on the Board of Alkyl Amines Chemicals Ltd, Artson Engineering and Aether Industries, all of them listed on the Bombay Stock Exchange

IIT Couples: Leja and Satish, Sulochana and Naresh Kapoor and Suman and Bharat Shiralkar

Life at IIT Bombay

On the first day, the IITB Director Prof. Bose gave a speech to all the 400 students joining that year to tell them 'you are the cream of the cream'. I was made to sit in the first row, right in the middle, bang under the director's nose. But I didn't mind because even in school I had the habit of always sitting in the front row.

> **IIT BOMBAY, TO ME IS: THE PLACE THAT GAVE ME EVERYTHING. I COULDN'T HAVE ASKED FOR MORE.**

Although I was the lone female in class, the guys were extremely helpful and friendly. I never felt awkward or left out. I remember the workshop class where we had carpentry, lathe and so on. When I struggled with forging - especially the heat - the guys would say, "Leja move aside, let us help you". Even today, my IIT classmates are among my best friends.

There were so few girls at IITB, we didn't even have a ladies hostel. A few staff residential quarters were given to us, and we had to share the bedrooms. We had two caretakers - Jana bai and Tara bai - who did the cooking and cleaning. It was such a homely atmosphere. It was like I was in my home.

I met my husband Satish at IIT. He walked into the class, I somehow liked him and we became friends, I was not so sure how my parents would accept him because we are Christians from Kerala. So we both got admission at the University of Massachusetts, went to the US and got married two months later. We have been married for more than fifty years. Both he and our son have supported me throughout my career.

Professional Journey

I started my career in 1975 with Tata Consulting Engineers and enjoyed every moment of it. Starting as a process engineer, I rose through the ranks and became a project manager. You went to the site and saw what you engineered come to reality and you helped in ironing out the glitches during the commissioning of the plant.

I had a long and satisfying career with the Tatas. Why did I leave? When the person heading Tata Consulting Engineers retired, I was interviewed for the position by the then TCE Chairman at Bombay House. The head of personnel of TCE, a Parsi gentleman, told me later that I didn't get selected because I am female. That was the only time my gender had a negative role in my entire career, and it was disappointing.

Satish used to say, "Leja, you're not married to TCE. Look for other opportunities". When Jacobs India approached me, I felt I would be a good fit with them. So I joined them in 2005 and I was there till I retired in 2014, as Vice President, Business Development. I learned a lot about international practices and Jacobs practices, which are exemplary, in those 10 years.

After retirement, I thought of pursuing my PhD, something I had always

Early days at IIT Bombay

Another holiday at the Grand Canyon

wanted. When I came to IITB and met Prof. Gudi and Prof. Kakkar (who was the Director at that time), Prof. Kakkar said, "Leja you don't need a PhD. You have so much experience, you should be teaching our students". I was offered an Adjunct Professorship and I accepted it.

RAPID FIRE

I believe: I can do anything.
I love: My husband and our son.
The world needs: Good human beings with ethical values.
I am passionate about: Everything that I do. I don't do things by half measures.
If you fall: Dust your knees and start up again.
Success is: A job well done.
My favorite song: "I am strong, I am invincible, I am woman…"

Teaching at IITB

In our time we had 60-65 students in a class. The professors knew each student by name. That is no longer possible. Today we have around 200 students. So it's a lecture theatre format and you have to use microphones and screens and all kinds of things to teach. It's moved from an intimate kind of setting to a more formal teaching style.

In our time, IIT didn't teach us how to make P&ID (Piping and Instrumentation Diagrams). I used to come for campus interviews when I was with the Tatas, as well as with Jacobs. I gave the institute feedback about industry requirements and we now teach Piping and Instrumentation Diagrams to students.

Teaching has been quite an experience but what I don't like is the 'crib sessions' for marks. There is a formal crib session where students compare papers and say, "Why did he get half a mark more. I wrote exactly the same thing!" And I say, "It's not the half mark that makes a difference in your life. Focus on learning the subject."

Challenges as a Woman

During my first project with TCE, I went for the commissioning of the plant. There were no bathrooms for women at the site. I'd go out there and say, "Guys, I'm here. So if you come out, I can use the loo". And they obliged. So, it was not a big deal. I didn't expect to get a separate washroom for a single female.

I never asked for special favors at the workplace. If you want to be treated as an equal, you have to accept the same work pressures as any man. When I was onsite for weeks or even months, I'm sure my family missed me as much as I missed them but that was the requirement of the job.

Work-Life Balance

I couldn't have done all the things that I did if it was not for the support from my husband and son. When I had to travel, I would just come from the office and tell Satish that I'm going to Japan because there's a meeting tomorrow. And he would say, "Okay, let's drop you to the airport". I was also fortunate to have in-laws who were most welcoming, though I was not the traditional 'Gori gomti' daughter-in-law!

I went onsite for six weeks but ended up staying nearly six months because during the commissioning of the plant, you are needed to sort things out. Those were the days we didn't have cell phones. Once when I came home, I found a little puppy in a basket. Satish said that our son Anand was feeling lonely, so he got him a dog.

Incidentally, both the men in my life are great cooks and we also enjoy eating out. Now that I have retired and have time on my hands, I am learning Indian classical music and playing the harmonium. Apart from teaching, I am on the board of 3 BSE listed companies and that keeps me well occupied.

Advice to Young Women

Don't ask for special favors. When the job has to be done, do it. Make sure you have a support system at home when you take up a job. Otherwise, there will be friction.

AWARDS & HONORS

- Second woman to graduate from the Chemical Engineering Department in IIT Bombay.
- Member of the board of three listed companies; and a senior member of the American Institute of Chemical Engineers.

ENGINEERING A BETTER WORLD

IIT Bombay took me from a shy young woman, gave me a voice and empowered me, and I'll always be grateful for that.

Early Life

I always wanted to be an engineer because my father was an engineer. He graduated just as India achieved independence and was involved in some very important infrastructure projects such as water supply and electrification networks. Sometimes, he would take me to a project before the formal inauguration, and let me turn on a light. I shared the excitement and sense of achievement.

I come from Goa and we didn't have electricity or piped water for many, many years. Now we have these comforts and so I've seen the impact of engineering on the lives of ordinary people in my village.

When the IIT entrance exam results were announced, I found that my name was not on the list. I was inconsolable and cried for three days. Then, a letter arrived stating that I had been admitted to IIT Bombay. It was just that my name had got cut while printing (it was the last line on the first page of the list!).

Life at IIT Bombay

It was a bit of a shock to see so few women at IIT. We were only 20 women in the then 'Ladies Hostel' and most were postgraduates. I wasn't prepared for the tough environment. I was not used to the vegetarian food. And the work was extremely difficult, I studied 14 to 15

DR. MARLENE KANGA AO

B.Tech, Chem Engg, 1976

Non-Executive Director - Sydney Water Corporation, Air Services Australia, Standards Australia; Past President - Engineers Australia and World Federation of Engineering Organisations; Past Board Member - Innovation Australia; IIT Bombay distinguished alumna, 2012; Officer of the Order of Australia

Dr Marlene Kanga with UNESCO Natural Sciences Division Director at WFEO 50th Anniversary and signing of UNESCO-WFEO Declaration on advancing the UN Sustainable Development Goals through engineering, Paris 7 March 2018

hours a day. But I think that prepared me, built my brain muscles, if you like. Everything else has been easy after that.

I became the mess secretary in my second year. I was determined to control costs and went around with a bunch of keys, handed out ingredients and so on. The women cooks used to have a good laugh because my Marathi was terrible but we established a good relationship and they became very protective. I must have done a good job because I was in charge for four years, until I graduated.

We used to routinely run out of rice and sugar because it was rationed. I thought, "I'll negotiate with the boys hostel" as they usually had a surplus. The boys were always after my lecture notes, which were detailed and good. So I would barter my lecture notes for some rice. In this way, I learned to deal with people, to negotiate, and that has stood me in very good stead.

Professional Journey

At IIT Bombay, I was taught environmental engineering by Prof. Indira Madhavan, one of the very few women professors in the faculty. That was where the idea of socially

Dr Marlene Kanga, as WFEO President, hosts the WFEO Annual Gala Dinner and Awards at the Institution of Civil Engineers, 1 King George Terrace, Westminster, London, October 2018

responsible engineering was seeded. I went on to complete a Master's in Chemical Engineering, specializing in process safety, from Imperial College, University of London and a PhD from Macquarie University in Australia.

When I first arrived in Australia, I sent hundreds of applications, to every chemical company in the Yellow Pages. I actually had to apply for jobs advertised under 'men' and 'boys'. When I got a job with Esso Australia I was only the second woman engineer that they'd ever hired. And I never looked back.

My field of work has been process safety engineering. I don't have any large edifices to point out to say, "I built that", but I know that I've kept millions in the community safe because of the work that I've done and that's empowering. I enjoy my work so much that even if they didn't pay me, I would do it.

> **THE POLITICIANS MAY TALK ABOUT IT, THE POLICYMAKERS MAY SAY THEY'RE GOING TO PAY FOR IT, BUT WHO IS GOING TO ACTUALLY DO IT? IT'S THE ENGINEERS WHO ARE GOING TO DEVELOP AND IMPLEMENT THE SOLUTIONS.**

Transforming Engineering Globally

In 2005, Engineers Australia called me to discuss 'women in engineering'. This started my new journey. I eventually became Chair of the National Committee for Women in Engineering, and organized the 'Year of Women in Engineering' in 2007, including a national conference for women from across the country. Many were working as the only woman in their team and were so happy to meet colleagues in the same company, and went on to form their own networks.

In 2011. I organized an international conference, a first for Australia and with travel awards from sponsors, which brought women engineers from around Asia. This was the inaugural INWES Asia Pacific Nation Network (APNN) meeting which resulted in nine women in engineering networks being established across Asia including India, Nepal, Sri Lanka and Bangladesh. We now have 19 such networks in the Asia-Pacific region and the APNN celebrated its 10th anniversary in 2021 in the Philippines.

I became the second woman (first Asian woman) to be President of Engineers Australia in its 94-year history in 2013. In 2015, I was elected President of the World Federation of Engineering Organisations (WFEO), which is like a 'UN of engineering', with members from 100 nations representing more than 30 million engineers. As President of WFEO in 2017-2019, I led the proposal for UNESCO to declare 'World Engineering Day for Sustainable Development' to be held every year, on 4th March.

This is the first and only UNESCO international day for engineering. In 2021, there were 300 events worldwide and we were able to reach 32 million people on social media.

As WFEO President, I also initiated and led a review of international engineering education benchmarks

Dr. Marlene Kanga with husband Dr. Rustom Kanga and sons Dr. Zubin Kanga and Dr. Jehan Kanga

Dr. Kanga announces approval by the UNESCO Member States of World Engineering Day at opening of World Engineers Convention, Melbourne Nov 2019

that were approved in 2021. This will transform engineering from the inside out, making it more inclusive, encouraging innovation and critical thinking, considerate of the impacts of engineering solutions for sustainable development and accessible to all.

RAPID FIRE

I believe: That engineers can change the world.
If I could, I would: Get more girls to become engineers.
I love: My family, my husband and my children and work.
I wish: I had more time in the day, 27 hours, perhaps.
If you fall: Make sure that you have a good friend or a partner to catch you.
The stuff I don't sweat: The little things, for example, I don't do any ironing.

Challenges as a Woman

I still face enormous barriers but I've got a thick skin. I just let it roll off because my sense of purpose is so strong that it drives me forward. Engineering workplaces have developed in a male-dominated environment. You find that even the most basic amenities for women don't exist, in particular in Australia. I'm advocating for those facilities and also for closing the gender pay gap, which still exists in Australia, even at entry level.

Work-Life Balance

A lot of young women struggle hard to have it all - very high-powered jobs as well as a young family and

children. And I say to them, life is not a race. Don't be in a rush to do it all at the same time. You can take a break from something and catch up later.

I was very passionate about my career and when I was pregnant, I'd gone to the board of my company and asked them to set up a childcare center. But when I had my first son, I just couldn't go back to full time work. I'm so glad I took a break for time with my children. They are with you for such a short time, which is so precious. I wasn't the perfect mother but I did my best, and like everything else, I did it with great passion and energy.

I set up a consulting business when my children were very young so that I had the flexibility to have time with my children, my parents-in-law and my mother. You can't put a price on that. Life is about everything, not just work. As a woman, you need to be a daughter, a sister, a mother, a wife and have good female friends and be a whole person. In my career, I've paced myself as if I am in a marathon.

So I still have a lot of energy and enthusiasm, I'm not burnt out.

Advice to Young Women

Engineering is essential for our modern world which needs roads, clean water, sanitation, communication. It is closely linked to the UN Sustainable Development Goals. As an engineer, you will acquire the skills to help make a better world, to improve people's lives. This is engineering with purpose. It is important for women to consider engineering as a career that makes a difference.

Also, in an increasingly technological world, it's important for women to contribute to engineering solutions. If the engineering team is 50-50 in terms of gender, the resulting solutions will be more relevant to the community.

Marlene (Fernandez) Kanga at the Ladies Hostel with her dog Trixie (visiting)

PROVING HER WORTH

I am often asked 'what is your dream job'? And my answer is, the job that I currently have.

Early Life

I grew up in suburban Mumbai. My father was an Accounts Officer with the Central Government. My mother was, and still is, a homemaker. As a kid, I was constantly asking how? What is this and why is this so? I devoured the 'Tell me why?' series of books. It was a very nerdy thing to do but I really enjoyed it and discussed it with my parents.

Academic excellence was very important in our family. I was always at the top of the class at St Mary's Convent School, Mulund. It was easy to believe that I can do whatever I want to do, and for this, I must also thank my mother. She constantly instilled in me self-belief.

In junior college, I dropped biology. And at that point, my father said, if not medicine, then you should do engineering. And if you are doing engineering, you have to get into IIT. Pursuit of excellence - nothing but the best! So I prepared for JEE, solved tons of Agrus problem sheets. It was challenging but genuinely fun.

We were on vacation when the result came out. When I got back, my neighbor had stuck a note on the door saying, "You have done well!" And that's when I came to know my All India Rank was 14. I took up computer science because I had a high rank, that's what all toppers do. And I knew no better!

Life at IIT Bombay

It was amazing, as a 17-year-old, to have unfettered freedom, living in a hostel. My fondest memories of IIT are the cack sessions in the wing and the night cafeteria. Also, the week-

DR. MEENA MAHAJAN

B.Tech, Computer Science, 1986

Professor, The Institute of Mathematical Sciences, Chennai

"Your self-belief is worth everything - hang on to it tightly!"

2014: Enjoying teaching

1994: With family at brother's wedding

> IIT BOMBAY, TO ME IS: WHERE MY JOURNEY BEGAN AS AN ADULT, AS A CITIZEN, AS A SCIENTIST

end hikes. Sitting in a cave or overlooking a lake - no light pollution, no sound pollution, just the stars in the sky. Chatting, singing, enjoying the beauty of nature.

In my first year, I went a bit berserk participating in extra-curriculars. During the inter-hostel freshers' competitions, I acted in two plays. Based on that, I was chosen to act in that year's Hindi annual production, 'Pagla Ghoda' by Badal Sarkar. Rehearsals went on Monday to Friday after dinner for three hours, for three months. The process was a complete revelation to me because we were all equal, sitting together, discussing how to present. Incidentally, I played four different female characters in that one play.

Initially, my grades were nothing to write home about. It took 3-4 semesters before I figured out a reasonable balance between doing extra-curriculars and giving attention to academics.

Professional Journey

By the time I finished my M.Tech. from IIT Bombay, I had dabbled with

1969: The world is my oyster!

hardware, software, networking, but didn't particularly enjoy any of it. So I thought, let me explore theoretical computer science, and enrolled for a PhD at IIT Madras in automata theory. I had an opportunity to audit a course in complexity theory and fell in love with it. I switched my research topic after completing my thesis, and it became my subsequent life long career.

One of the things that I'm working on right now is proof complexity, which is totally fascinating. What we are doing is we are looking at statements which are obviously false e.g. 50 students join IIT. They have to be assigned rooms in a hostel which has 40 rooms. It's clear to you and me that everybody will not go to single rooms. But a proof of such a statement, written in many formats, is humongously difficult for programs to check.

Complexity theory is about formally proving what cannot be done, what are the limits of computation. Nowadays, every smartphone is a pretty powerful computer, yet we are worrying about how much disk storage we have. Is that enough for the kind of code we want to run? Somebody has to tell the designers that beyond this point, do not aim to try and optimize further. The big buzz word is 'lower bounds'.

My research interests also include algebraic complexity, counting classes, circuit complexity, and its connections to automata. I enjoy teaching courses about Boolean function complexity and concrete lower bounds.

Challenges as a Woman

When I was a student at IIT, I decided that I'm here to make the most of it, and the fact that I am a woman and not a man does not matter. I was the only computer science student in H10, in my batch. Many of my classmates would sit together and solve assignments whereas I was doing them alone. But that didn't bother

1985: Bonhomie in the department

me. It's really a question of allowing external circumstances to make a difference vs not allowing them.

At IIT Madras it was even less of an issue because by then I was already doing PhD and my advisor Dr. Kamala Krithivasan is also a woman. At IMSc, where I do my teaching and research, I have been fortunate and never experienced any kind of bias.

RAPID FIRE

I believe: That my actions make a difference in the world.
If I could, I would: Spend more time in the hills
I love: Reading, especially well-crafted fiction.
The world needs? Liberal doses of kindness and empathy and gentle humor.
I'm passionate about: My teaching.
The stuff I don't sweat: Culinary disasters.

Work-Life Balance

You imagine this balance between scales - work on one side and life on the other. I cannot resonate with that at all because my work is something I enjoy so much; it is part of life, not versus life.

Each one finds his or her own way, but my way has been to always keep

a distinction between 'important' and 'urgent'. You try to make sure that there are not too many urgent things that impinge on your time and distract you from doing what is important and what matters. For me, it's never been a question of sacrifice. It's a question of choices. When my kids were very young, I did not travel to workshops and conferences or for collaborations. Maybe if I had travelled more I would have had one and a half times as many publications by now. Does that make me any less successful? I don't think so.

Advice to Young Women

The main thing I would say is 'stick to the plan'. Just believe. You know that you want to do this. Don't let anybody else tell you otherwise. There are places, points in time, when it's going to be hard. It's hard for everybody. You may feel it's hard for you because you're a woman. It's hard for men also, in a different way. Just don't think about it.

Your self-belief is worth everything - hang on to it tightly!

AWARDS & HONORS

- Fellow of the Indian Academy of Sciences.
- A member of the Editorial Board of the Leibniz International Proceedings in Informatics.
- On the Advisory Board of the journal TheoretiCS.
- An editor of the journal Logical Methods in Computer Science.
- On the Board of Trustees for the Computational Complexity Conference
- Member of the Council of IARCS, the Indian Association for Research in Computer Science.
- Member of several program committees such as MFCS 2022, SAT 2022, SAT2021, CSR2020, IARSC21-23, STACS2020.
- An ACM India Eminent Speaker giving talks on computability and complexity.

"No matter where you start, many possibilities are open to you."
PARK

MOTHER OF INVENTIONS

It's the melding and blending of disciplines that will propel us into the future.

Early Life

I grew up in Mumbai, where I studied in an all-girls school (St. Columba). I loved languages and social studies, as well as physics and mathematics, so I considered all of these subjects for higher studies. Although my father and grandfather were engineers, there was no female engineer in the family. Thus, even with this background, engineering felt like forging a new path.

I would have been content to stay at home and attend a local engineering school. But my mother pushed me to prepare for IIT. She said, "You can do it. I know you can. Give it your best shot!" I will always be grateful for that, as coming to IIT Bombay completely changed my life.

Life at IIT Bombay

I have fond memories of midnight treasure hunts, cracking cryptic crossword clues, quiz competitions but dramatics was closest to my heart. I took part in dramatics all five years, represented H10, and actually got the top prize for Best Actor in my final year.

When I came into IIT, I was influenced not just by my peer group, but by the senior women in the hostel who held very bold and progressive views. When I was a freshie, they broke the rule of 'no male visitors' allowed in the hostel. I was in awe of what they were doing, how they went to the director and said 'no double standards'.

DR. MUKTA FAROOQ

B.Tech, Metallurgical Engineering and Materials Science, 1983

IBM Distinguished Research Staff Member
Heterogeneous Integration Leader at IBM Research
IBM Lifetime Master Inventor with 230 Granted US Patents

Shaji, Mukta, Priya, Sameer celebrating Sameer's First Birthday, New York, USA, May 1995

But to be honest, the single most important influence in my life was my classmate (and now husband) Shaji Farooq. In my 3rd year at IIT, I moved to the Metallurgical Engineering Department and so did Shaji. We met in a cool, open hallway on the first day of our fifth semester. And the rest is history.

Professional Journey

When I came to the US, I first did my Master's at Northwestern, assessing aluminium zirconium alloys – very traditional metallurgy. Then

Mukta at Northwestern University, Evanston, USA, November 1983

> **IIT BOMBAY, TO ME IS: A PLACE THAT SHAPED AND DEFINED ME.**

I moved to Rensselaer Polytechnic Institute for my PhD, as I wanted to start looking at semiconductor materials. As part of my doctoral thesis, I actually built Schottky devices from scratch, and fell in love with this field.

Truly, it is the perfect blend of three extraordinary disciplines – solid state physics, material science, and electronics. My field is called Heterogeneous Integration. We are trying to find unique, innovative solutions that will overcome the slowing down of logic scaling because, as chips are getting faster and better, they're also coming up against some roadblocks.

What I'm doing is leading a team that looks for innovative methods to overcome this slowing down and bring new solutions to the forefront. There are multiple ways of doing this, so it's heterogeneous. It's not the old 'one size fits all'.

Inventor Mindset

At IBM, I was placed with a group working on groundbreaking semiconductor packaging technology. As the youngest team member, my job was to run the hardware, evaluate it and inspect it. This gave me a real feel for the problem we were trying to solve. I realized there was a way to make the process simpler and less prone to defects.

When I shared this with the senior engineers, they got excited and said, "This is a very important idea". That's how my idea was incorporated into patent # US 5,266,446. It was thrilling to have my name on a patent! Ruminating on unsolved problems and looking for new solutions became a way of life for me.

As an inventor, you look at a solution which is good, but then you ask - can I do it another way? And then you come up with two other ways, and one or both of them may end up becoming key Intellectual Property. Of my 230 granted patents, 40 plus got recognized with company awards, but many more became part of the technology manufacturing process. I led the team at IBM which achieved the industry's first ever high volume logic wafer with through silicon vias – that was truly exhilarating!

Work-Life Balance

Shaji and I came to the US, got married, got our PhDs together and started working at IBM on the same day. So, in a way, we've had parallel ca-

Sameer, Mukta, Shaji, Priya at Shaji's NYU MBA Valedictorian Commencement, New York, USA, May 1999

Mukta in her doctoral cap and gown, ready to hood Sameer, at the MD Commencement Ceremony, Boston University, Boston USA, May 2018.

RAPID FIRE

I love: That first morning on vacation, when you're waking up to a blank calendar.
The world needs: More acts of kindness and caring.
I'm passionate about: Helping those less fortunate.
The stuff I don't sweat: I don't sweat anything, except health.
Success is: Being happy with where you are in life.
One thing I wish somebody had told me when I was 18: Go ahead and do your thing – it may be different, weird, crazy, but it will be 'you'.

reers. Although we've always been a bit competitive with each other (some parts of IIT never leave you), we've always encouraged each other to excel.

Once we had children, the equation changed because now we were a family. And so, there were times when we would pick up slack for each other. In the early 90s, there had been big layoffs in material science so we decided to diversify our careers. In the fall of '95, Shaji started doing an MBA in Finance from NYU Stern, while he was still at IBM. This was a crazy period. He would come back in the middle of the night and work on his MBA projects, while I was looking after two young kids while still working full-time at IBM.

I saw women at work quitting in droves, not able to handle their careers along with their familial demands, deciding that staying home would let them preserve their sanity. It was tempting. But Shaji would not hear of it. He said that I was capable of great things in my career, and that he would not let me quit after all the academic successes under my belt, and all the hard work I had already put in. He said that to give it up midstream would be a regret that would haunt me for the rest of my life. This much is true: he knew me better than I knew myself.

And he was not just an armchair husband who made philosophical observations but refused to lift a finger! He pulled his own weight and then some. If I was bathing the kids, he was right there, helping me. If I was doing grocery shopping or ferrying the children to soccer or tennis, he was at home cooking. If I was doing errands on a weeknight, he was helping the kids with math or physics. And he was right. The hardest, craziest times did pass. And my career, which at times demanded so much and made my life so hard, eventually proved to be a sustaining force that made me happy and fulfilled.

Challenges as a Woman

At IIT, we were just 6 women in a class of 300 guys, but that skewed ratio gave me the ability to hold my own. Maybe it's not always comfortable, but I think getting out of my comfort zone and saying, I'm going to stand there and deal with the proverbial brickbats – that was a lesson for life.

For years, I used to be the only female engineer in so many meetings. Not to mention that I was in a different culture in the US! But due to my IIT experience, I felt confident standing up and saying, "I think we should do it this way and I'll tell you why."

Advice to Young Women

A career in STEM takes hard work. But whether in materials science or electronics or AI, you can do things which will bring tremendous benefits to human society.

As a high schooler, you may not know which discipline you want to pursue, sometimes it just takes time for it to unfold. No matter where you start; many possibilities are open to you.

AWARDS & HONOURS

- IEEE EPS Outstanding Sustained Technical Contribution Award (2022)
- IEEE Technological Innovation Award (Region 1 - 2021)
- Distinguished Alumna of IIT Bombay (2017)
- IEEE Fellow (2016)
- Outstanding Technical Achievement Award for 3D Integration (2015)
- IBM Academy of Technology (2014)

DESIGN MATTERS

My feminist consciousness is always alert while designing spaces.

Early Life

I was fortunate to grow up in a liberal, cosmopolitan and secular environment in Bombay, in the post-independence era. My father was a freedom fighter, government official, and a social activist at heart. As part of his job in the Education and Culture department, he addressed social issues like alcoholism among textile mill workers, using local cultural forms. As a school going girl, I often accompanied him.

My mother's father was an educationist. He started one of the early schools for girls called Sharda Sadan, in Girgaon area, through the Aryan Education Society. My mother got married at the age of 19 but continued her graduation studies after marriage. Her own father insisted on paying her fees.

My parents met while they were part of a theatre group called the Indian National Theatre which produced progressive plays. My parents encouraged me to develop an interest in the arts, dance and theatre. I entered the field of architecture for my graduation. Coincidentally, I met my life partner, Arvind, while acting in a play at the JJ College of Architecture.

While the cultural environment in JJ was lively, the academic courses were trapped in a century old, inward looking colonial syllabus. The syllabus was drafted by the British, mainly to train the students to become draftsmen for assisting the British architects. The B.Arch. course was focused mainly on structure and construction, rather than on designing spaces conducive for evolving human habitation.

My father wanted me to go abroad for my postgraduate studies but I knew

NEERA ADARKAR

Industrial Design Centre (IDC), 1974

Architect, Urbanist, Adarkar Associates
Founder Trustee and Chairperson, School of Environment and Architecture, SEA

"The days of creating ivory towers are over."

he couldn't afford it. After a year of working in an architectural office, I heard about the Industrial Design course which had just opened in IIT. What was fascinating to me was its multidisciplinary content - visual design, film making, photography and some exposure to research.

In early teens

Life at IIT Bombay

The IDC faculty was young and enthusiastic. Unlike JJ College of Architecture, the hierarchy between students and teachers was blurred.

With partner Arvind Adarkar

It was a different classroom experience for me with a lot of hands-on work. One of my design projects was based on my mother's research. She had developed a methodology using phonetics to teach children who were first-generation learners. I designed an interactive kit to further enhance the process of learning.

School for Environment and Architecture, SEA

Living in the hostel was also an exhilarating experience for me. I made friends from other disciplines and other regions outside Maharashtra and traveled with them on short trips. The film club introduced me to serious cinema. Most importantly, I got my first exposure to gender consciousness in the IIT hostel, through some students who were more politically conscious than me. The concept of a collective movement was introduced to me during my stint in IIT.

Interestingly, my various exposures in the IIT campus added new layers to my relationship with my partner Arvind. He was already aware of my consciousness as an independent woman but to see it as a part of a larger struggle was an important step

"

IIT BOMBAY, TO ME IS: A SPACE WHICH OPENED MY WORLD VIEW.

for him too. Our participation in the experimental Hindi and Marathi theatre and exposure to world cinema through the newly emerging film clubs made our lives vibrant with new thinking and ideas.

Arvind had already set up an architectural practice. I tried to look for jobs as a fresh 'Product Designer' from IDC but the economy was not global yet and 'design' was looked through a narrow lens of 'beautification'. So, a mechanical engineer was always preferred to an architect. Meanwhile, I joined two colleges of architecture as visiting faculty.

I realized that architecture and urbanism offered a wider horizon in multiple genres. This made me join Arvind as his professional partner.

Professional Journey

As architects, we have designed buildings, mostly institutional works and housing. But we also engage in heritage planning and urban research work. My professional journey is not independent from my personal journey. Our involvement in urban movements like housing, women's rights, the struggle for demanding the land under the defunct textile mills for public use etc, has informed our approach towards all our studio projects.

Similarly, my feminist consciousness is always alert while designing spaces. Before I became a part of the larger women's movement, I always thought that the discipline of architecture is 'neutral'. But soon I realized that the physical spaces have a great influence on social relationships. Some of us women architects then formed a group called 'Women Architects Forum'. Collectively, we started looking at built spaces through a gender perspective.

At present, the IIT Bombay alumni is funding a new women's hostel on the Mumbai campus. As one of the constituent members of the Hostel Building Committee, I ensured that the brief for the new hostel was sensitive to gender requirements. A

Awarded Honorary Doctorate from Katholieke University, Belgium

Speech after receiving Distinguished Alumnus Award, IIT Bombay 2013

well-designed housing space can improve and inculcate a sense of community living.

We created an affordable mass housing project of 5000 tenements called the Nagari Niwara Trust. Apart from regular amenities, we made provision for a creche, a school and a women's center. Years later, I am proud to say that the community spaces are used in innovative and vibrant manners.

In 2013, my partner Arvind took an initiative to start a new undergraduate school of architecture by bringing together a group of eight like-minded and thinking architects as the founder trustees. It is called 'School of Environment and Architecture, or SEA. Unfortunately, Arvind did not live to see the school, which opened in 2014.

SEA is known today as a very stimulating academic space. It consciously engages the students with the city and the society at large through research, advocacy and space design. I am one of the Founder Trustees and the Chairperson of SEA.

RAPID FIRE

I believe: In the Constitution.
If I could, I would: Live the same life again.
The world needs: Ethics and Empathy.
One thing I wish somebody had told me when I was 18: To be optimistic.
The most important thing to remember when I step into work: See it as an extension of your personal life.

Challenges as a Woman

No woman can say that she is free from any challenges arising from gender bias especially in the public sphere. She cannot live a completely free, uninhibited life. In my working sphere, it was initially difficult for government officials to see me conducting meetings on my own. But I can say that in my personal and professional life. I did not suffer a setback because of my gender.

This is mainly because of the confidence I developed from my liberal family upbringing and my participation in the women's movement quite early in life. Yes, in the early years, the clients did expect Arvind as the 'boss' for final decisions, but it was just a matter of days... As I mentioned earlier, being surrounded by my frequently visiting feminist friends, I could see my partner's efforts to grow (as close as possible for a man) towards feminism.

When my mother had to go through a painful divorce, Arvind was her closest confidante and later when she had severe Alzheimer's disease, as a caregiver, he truly played the role of her 'mother'.

Work-Life Balance

When my mother and Arvind's mother needed daily caregiving, we first thought of a combined work and home space. Later, we bought a larger place and took our turns as caregivers. The most challenging phase was when my mother needed constant attention. On the days the caregiver would be absent, we have held meetings at home.

My mother's constant roaming around in the house - a repetitive activity which is linked to Alzheimer's - would sometimes prove a disturbance to our meetings, but soon guests had to get used to it. The division between private and public is not impermeable, in fact it is quite porous.

Message to Young Women

Just because STEM deals with science and technology, it should not be disconnected with someone's personal and social life. As architects, we are fortunate to interact directly with the users of the spaces we design. Similarly, STEM professionals (across genders) should establish a dialogue, a conscious effort to connect with society at large.

There is a larger world - real, more vibrant and innovative beyond the corporate world. During the pandemic, many boundaries have become less defined, especially between the workplace and home space. The new professionals should demystify the aura around STEM. The days of creating ivory towers are over.

Especially in the current social context, it is very important to challenge various discriminations existing not only in the field of work but beyond. It is our responsibility to make our respective worlds more inclusive, especially educational campuses like the IITs.

Awards and Honors

- Distinguished Alumnus Award, IIT Bombay, 2013.
- Honorary Doctorate, KU Leuven University, Belgium 2014.

BOOKS AUTHORED BY NEERA ADARKAR

1. 'MultipliCITIES: Urban Cultures of the Mumbai Metropolitan Region', published by Mumbai Metropolitan Region: Heritage Conservation Society, 2020.
2. 'One Hundred Years One Hundred Voices, Oral History of Millworkers of Girangaon' (co-authored with Meena Menon), Seagull Kolkata, 2004.
3. 'The Chawls of Mumbai: Galleries of Life', ImprintOne, New Delhi, 2011.

Working in the lab is fun

"Try to experience and explore as much as possible."

SWADESI SCIENTIST

Wet lab experiments in biology may be slow but the work is futuristic and exciting.

Early Life

I belong to Udaipur, which is this small town in Rajasthan. I did my schooling from St Mary's Convent until 8th grade and finished 12th grade from Maharana Mewar Public school, set up in a horse stable of the palace of the city.

My father had started a small cattle feed company but since he was also holding a job, my mother took it over and ran the business. She was a hard-working lady who managed both work and a family with three kids quite well. I would see her running around all the time, making sure that our needs were met in terms of food and studies. She is one of my biggest inspirations.

There were only two options for good students back then. You go for medical studies or engineering. Although my parents wanted me to become a doctor, I felt that I had to follow a trend set by my father and elder brothers, who are all graduates from various IITs. And when I saw my elder brother preparing for JEE, he became my role model. I said, "I want to do the same thing."

Life at IIT Bombay

I was the only girl in the Metallurgical Engineering class of 45 students. There was no fixed seating. I would sit alone on an entire bench, every day. I was also quite shy, which made things worse. The feeling of isolation affected my academics, apart from other things.

In the 4th year, after we had gone on a couple of industry visits, I got to know my classmates better and overcame my inhibitions. I started feeling more 'myself'. The girls who come to IIT today are so much more fortunate - they are a big gang in their respective classes now.

DR. PRAKRITI TAYALIA

B.Tech, Metallurgical Engineering and Materials Science, 1999

Associate Professor, Department of Biosciences and Bioengineering, IIT Bombay

My darling daughters

IIT BOMBAY, TO ME IS: EVERYTHING, AT THIS POINT OF TIME.

Luckily in the hostel, I had very good friends (Rachna and Vaishnavi) - we would eat, drink, sleep, fight, cry and laugh together. Best memories were going to the coffee shack for Maggi or Maggi bonda, or to the middle gate at 11 in the night to buy biscuits and junk food.

In my 3rd year, I participated in the Inter-IIT sports meet held at Kharagpur. We put together women's basketball team just a month before the tournament. I still remember the slogans from our cheering squad during the sports meet!

I also met my future husband, Dinesh Balachandran, at IITB. He was my classmate and from the same department. We got married six years after graduating from IIT. When we visited the campus after the wedding with a box of sweets, a couple of our professors indicated that they were aware of our courtship :).

I did not have a stellar academic record in my department, however, when I did my Seminar and B.Tech. project with Prof. M.P. Dixit and Prof. T.R. Rama Mohan respectively, I realized that academics is more than just attending classes and preparing for exams. This is when I got a glimpse of research through reading some journal papers and doing some wet lab experiments.

Professional Journey

After my undergrad, I had a short stint in a software company and soon figured out that is not what I

Patience pays - nice to be rewarded for all the effort put in by our team

wanted to do. I went on to do my Master's in Materials Science from the University of Delaware and that's when I got interested in academics again and was exposed to the research aspect of it.

My Master's project involved developing a sensor that was modelled as an electrical circuit having resistive and inductive components and was validated with experiments. I realized that I liked doing wet lab experiments and wanted to work more in the field of materials. I decided to apply for PhD and went on to pursue it at Harvard in the broad area of Applied Physics and Bioengineering.

My PhD journey at Harvard also started in an unconventional manner. I had written up a project which was based on a technique called two photon polymerisation, a sort of 3D printing technique. I approached Prof. Eric Mazur, who was working in this area and I told him that I would like to apply this technique in the field of biology. He was a Professor in the Physics department and was equally excited when I discussed my idea with him. He gave

Chilling with family

Meet my lab – they keep the curiosity and energy flowing

me full freedom to work on it.
Coincidentally, just that year, Prof. David Mooney from University of Michigan Ann Arbor moved to Harvard's Bioengineering Department. So we collaborated with him and I started my career at the intersection of Physics and Biology.

RAPID FIRE

I believe: In being honest and truthful and being very upfront.
I love: Playing table tennis, although I'm not very good at it.
The world needs a bit more levity.
I'm passionate about: Trying to keep fit.
Success is: Being able to get a good night's sleep
One thing I wish somebody had told me when I was 18: Explore and experience as much as possible.
The most important thing when I step into work: Be an example for what you expect from others.

After finishing my PhD and post-doctoral stint at Harvard, my husband and I decided to move closer to our families in India, despite having green cards. At the same time, we were also clear that we would return only if I got a position at IIT Bombay. Once that was confirmed, we moved back permanently.

Frontiers of Science

I have set up the Cell and Tissue Engineering lab at IIT Bombay, wherein we use materials to do application-oriented work in the field of biology. We are developing material-based platforms for tissue engineering, immunotherapy and 3D in vitro models for drug-screening and understanding cellular mechanisms in diseased and pathological conditions.
For tissue engineering, 3D printing is currently the most advanced technique which allows incorporation of cells and matrices required to build a tissue or an organ outside the human body. In 5 to 10 years,

Harvard Commencement – A fantastic journey ended with a crown on my head

we may see complete organs grown outside the body and implanted in humans.

In our lab, we are working on skin tissue engineering, as well as cancer and auto-immune diseases. To take our technology to the next level, it needs to be tested on larger animals and human trials need to be conducted.

Wet lab experiments in the field of biology may be slow and need to be extremely methodical. However, the anticipated outcome of our research keeps us going and makes it exciting for us to work!

Work-Life Balance

I have two daughters, 8 and 12 years old. Managing home and career has never been very easy. One of the two always takes a hit at any point of time. However, my husband and I try to balance spending time with kids and have organically divided our tasks with respect to that.

Challenges as a Woman

I do not remember having any female professor in my own department when studying at IIT and a couple that I knew were in the Humanities Department. Today, the ratio of female to male professors has certainly improved, however, parity may be a distant dream.

I haven't faced any issues owing to my gender yet, though I wonder if I might have become blind to them or accepted them over so many years of being in minority. Academic life is rigorous, no matter where you are. Apart from being good at teaching and research, one has to excel at the art of multi-tasking.

Advice to Young Women

Try to experience and explore as much as possible. It's hard to decide or know initially what one wants to do, but as you go along you will find something of interest. Just follow through – and then leave no stone unturned to pursue.

SIGNAL MINDED

In my field, it is quite easy to motivate students because it's so highly applied.

Early Life

I grew up in Bombay in the suburb of Bandra. My father was a journalist while my mother was a medical practitioner. My parents, younger brother and I lived together with uncles and aunts, speaking multiple languages, given that my parents hailed from Karnataka and Gujarat, respectively.

I went to Bai Avabai Petit Girls' High School and I was the studious kind, who always did well in exams. In those days, if you were bright, you picked science and chose either medicine or engineering. My mother happened to be a doctor, in fact, everyone on her side of the family was in the medical profession. So that was the natural path for me.

As it happened, I did appear for medical college entrance and did not make it. I was disappointed but also relieved. In my heart, I knew I wasn't really cut out for it! And then, my friends told me about IIT JEE. I ended up sitting for that exam without much preparation. My rank was 154 (highest amongst girls in the zone).

I chose IIT Bombay and electrical engineering without a clue about what lay ahead. It was really a series of accidents that brought me to IIT rather than any strategy or plan!

Life at IIT Bombay

As a student, I can't say that I had a good time on campus. There were very few girls so you always tended to stand out, whether it was within class or outside of it. You had to deal with all kinds of isolation and the difficulties of not having a group to help you along. I remained shy and aloof throughout.

I did enjoy discovering the different areas of electrical engineering and even the courses in the humanities. One of the nice experiences, making for great memories, was joining the

DR. PREETI RAO

B.Tech, Electrical Engineering, 1984

Professor, Department of Electrical Engineering, IIT Bombay

"Take the time to investigate... till you find what you really want to do."

Family photo at Gir

The Silver jubilee reunion of batch of 1984 with Preeti's family in bottom right.

famous 'Himankan' treks on two occasions, organised by IITB's mountaineering club.

Somewhere along the way, I developed an interest in signal processing. Prof. Shankar taught analog signal processing while Prof. Kekre (CS dept) offered digital signal processing as an advanced / PG elective. This is now all in the core UG EE curriculum.

I realize I was privileged to have a very special educational experience but honestly, I was quite happy when the five years ended. It felt like being released from prison, almost. I never thought I'd come back! But life has a way of surprising you.

Professional Journey

I completed my PhD in signal processing from the University of Florida, Gainesville and my postdoc research at the University of Illinois, Urbana Champaign. After a brief visiting researcher stint at the Hitachi Central Research Labs in Tokyo, Japan, I joined IIT Kanpur as an Assistant Professor, following my husband Mahesh Patil (also IITB batch of 1984) in the same position.

Initially, I was a nervous wreck because I wasn't sure if I could handle the very competitive group of sharp IIT UG students.I will never forget how he quietly walked with me to the door of my first encounter with my tutorial batch of 3rd year UGs. I was behaving like I was walking into a den of lions. Over time, I became more comfortable in class but I was on the lookout for an industry

job. However, there were hardly any opportunities in the corporate sector and no straightforward entry path into government labs. So, when the IITB position came up a few years later, I decided to move closer to home.

When I joined, even the classrooms looked exactly like we had left them. All the big changes started happening after that. Today we have more female professors, more female students. There is a conscious effort on the part of IIT to be more balanced and engage with society. So it's been a completely different and positive experience being here again.

Bringing Tech to Life

My expertise is in the area of signal processing, which is a bunch of mathematical tools and methods applicable in different domains. Whenever there is information to be extracted, you use a signal. Humans use voice and images, for example. Machines interact with these signals in order to extract information and make sense of it, so that people can interact more naturally with computers.

With SensiBol team in 2011

EE department faculty and students

It's all the more visible now because we talk a lot about IOT. All our little devices interact with the world at large and to do that, they interface through signals. So whether they are sound signals or radio signals or temperature signals, everything is essentially being sensed via signals. In this field, it is quite easy to motivate students because it's just so highly applied. My interest lies in audio signal processing that involves sound and the human perception of it. I work on research problems in that area. As a professor, one has a chance to influence young minds, infect them with a zest for the subject and see them make excellent contributions.

RAPID FIRE

I believe: Everyone can contribute.
So if I could, I would: Pack more time into my schedule.
The world needs: People who are honest and committed
I'm passionate about: Making a meaningful difference.

I've also had the opportunity to co-found Sensibol Audio Technologies along with some of my students - Vishweshwara Rao, Sachin Pant, Sujeet Kini and Nagesh Nayak. In fact, Vishweshwara was a musician who had the dilemma of choosing a career in music or engineering. At the startup, he was able to combine both. To commercialise a technology you need a problem to solve. We built

some neat prototypes and demonstrations of a software that could evaluate a person's singing skills. When we gave demos at the IIT Alumni celebrations and so on, there was a lot of interest. So we formed a company called Sensibol in 2011.

We have had a number of interesting deployments of our singing, scoring and audio-mixing product. With music licensing being such a challenge in India, the company engaged mostly in services for the entertainment industry rather than taking on the challenges and promoting their own products.

Work-Life Balance

My mother was always a working woman so that concept was not new to me. My husband, Mahesh, is also my colleague in the same IIT department, so he could easily understand my need to do certain things, or spend a lot of time in my lab. I have never had to explain to my family why I was poring over my computer all the time. An interesting outcome is that my son Pranay wants to be a professor some day.

Advice to Young Women

There are a lot of opportunities and I think it's worth taking the time to investigate what's out there till you find what you really want to do.

Speaking at a conference at Rourkela

A Covid Thanksgiving – at home with family

"Success is transient... it's all about having fun getting there."

Radha and Chris before our wedding – so young!

Back when I was still taller than my kids! Bobby's elementary school graduation

RIDING THE WAVE

A semiconductor wafer is beautiful, it's like a piece of art.

Early Life

My father was an IAS officer (Karnataka cadre), he joined the service in 1952, soon after independence. One of his dreams was that in his lifetime, every hut in every village would have at least one electric light bulb. And I think that my mother shared that mindset. She was a housewife but always had something going on in parallel, some kind of volunteer work.

Although a mathematics graduate herself, my mom was very keen that one of us become a doctor and serve people. It was disappointing for her when that didn't happen. But I don't think that we felt pressure to be a particular way. We are four siblings - one brother and three sisters. My older brother and one of my sisters went to IIT Madras. They kind of set the bar quite high!

As the youngest in the family, I was, of course, inspired by them to aim high. But also, I truly loved math and science, thanks to my teachers in Sophia High School, Bangalore. Although I was a good student, I think I was a bit lazy. Studying for JEE (with the help of Agrawal postal notes) was the first time I really worked hard and long-term for some goal.

In 1991, my father was appointed as a Deputy Governor of the Reserve Bank, which was headquartered in Bombay. So, I decided to go to IIT Bombay. In the end, I only went home about once every two months, because we had such a close and supportive group in the hostel – but it was nice to know I could get home in a couple of hours if I wanted to.

Life at IIT Bombay

The gender ratio at IIT was quite a shock, coming from an all-girls school. In Chemical Engineering, we had more women than in most other

DR. RADHA NAYAK

B.Tech, Chemical Engineering, 1991

Vice President of Business Development and Marketing at LAM Research

All dressed up for the 25th reunion of the Class of 1991

> **IIT BOMBAY, TO ME IS: THE PLACE I WOKE UP AND BEGAN TO KNOW MYSELF.**

branches. But I still found it quite forbidding. I remember my three lab partners were passionately discussing a point about a fluid mechanics project. And I was thinking - they're on the wrong track. But it was hard for me to say it to them.

In my 4th year, I became the first girl to stand for Institute Literary Secretary. I couldn't have done it without the support of my wing in the hostel. During the campaign, some folks came up to me and said, "I really admire what you're doing". But this one time, in H7 I think, people threw tomatoes at me! Luckily I had a safe space to come back to with the women in my wing.

As Lit Sec, I am quite proud of some of the things we did – inventing new styles of crosswords for the Mood Indigo competitions, setting a challenging treasure hunt (which was a much-anticipated annual event), organizing inter-hostel competitions and in one of our magazine editions, challenging some decisions the faculty had made.

On the academic front, in my 2nd year we had 'Intro to Transport Phenomena' with Prof. Uday Shenoy. He was a new prof, young and very enthusiastic who made math and physics come together in a magical way! I stayed in Fluid Mechanics through my 3rd year and B.Tech. projects with Prof. Karthik Khilar and Prof. Devang Khakhar, and continued in that field in my PhD at MIT.

Professional Journey

I admit I was a bit terrified at MIT at first but I found that my IIT education stood me in good stead and the coursework wasn't too much for me. What I did find was that unlike in undergrad, in grad school, no one tells you what to do. If you spend a week and don't progress on your research, no one will question it. So the last couple of years of my PhD is when I learnt to be self-driven.

I met my partner, Chris, at MIT. He played a lot of sports (which I did not, and hence found kind of cool!), but we also read a lot of the same books and were science fiction nerds. Although Irish American, he had the same idea of family being important, so our values are very similar. As our careers progressed together, we both compromised equally to make it work for the other.

During my PhD program, I developed finite element methods for modelling complex liquid crystalline polymer flows. In essence, it is about mathematically describing the behavior of liquids (polymer solutions) that flow in odd ways – very differently from water – so that you can predict how they will behave when you process them in a factory to make polymer products.

From then on, almost my entire career has been in the semiconductor industry. In my first job at Applied Materials, I led a team of engineers in technology development and customer demonstrations, culminating in the release of the division's first 300mm wafer processing platform.

Making Things Better

Eventually, I became interested in the 'big picture', and moved to the marketing and business side. I worked with Novellus and then with Soraa, an LED startup. This stint was very important to me for two reasons. First, LEDs can cut electricity usage by 80% (and I link this back to my father's wish that one day, every village will have a light bulb). LEDs can make it possible.

Second, the startup environment is so energizing – there is so much built up from nothing and you develop so many diverse skills. I think I left Soraa as a much more effective leader and change agent, than when I joined. In addition, our founder won the Nobel Prize in Physics – it was truly a thrill to know him and work with such a high caliber of people in my time there.

Currently, I am with LAM Research, which is one of the largest suppliers of semiconductor equipment. We are

Truly best friends forever – go Hostel 10!

like the 'printing press' of the semiconductor world. No matter what kind of chip you're using in a phone or car or toaster, my equipment has participated in that.

I love the act of making things and that there's something physical. I remember, earlier in my career, bringing home semiconductor wafers, just one of them costs millions of dollars. But these were things we'd done in the lab and I find them very beautiful. Like a piece of art. I took one home to my parents and it was such a thrill, to say, "Hey, I made a part of this."

Work-Life Balance

Before I was a mom, too much of my self-worth was tied up in my work. And that made the stakes very high. So if it came to asking for a promotion, I got way too wound up inside myself. Post-motherhood, I acquired a completely separate area where I was needed. So I found that I was able to sit down and have conversations with my boss about my next career steps.

Nobel prize winners are people too... with Soraa Founder Shuji Nakamura

RAPID FIRE

I believe that: Perfection is overrated.
If I could I would: Have made myself more uncomfortable earlier in my life.
I love: Solving things.
The world needs: To change its shape for women and not expect women to change their shape for it.
I wish: I could live 3 different lives in one lifetime!
If you fall, you're not alone. Everyone who's done anything worthwhile has fallen multiple times.
The stuff I don't sweat: The idea of winning
One thing I wish somebody had told me when I was 18: That most of the things you need to learn in life, you won't learn in school.

I went through several waves in my career. There were three separate times where I just stayed in a job because I knew it wasn't the right time to move. My kids were not the right age, or I was going to have my second child, or my daughter needed me because she was having a tough time in elementary school.

You see women like Sheryl Sandberg and Marissa Mayer who, apparently, never slowed down. But for the vast majority of us, it's important to know that there is a time to be really focused on your career and there is a time to prioritize other things. At 52, my kids, my career, my volunteer work and my parents, all of those are things that really matter to me. I also make time to read, practice yoga, solve crossword puzzles and stay connected to my friends.

Challenges as a Woman

Women don't have enough role models to learn from. I spent a good bit of

Turning 50!! 2019 Hostel 10 Wing reunion in the Big Apple

my thirties thinking about how I appeared to the world, what it takes to convince people and be effective. Some people find me coming on 'too strong' while others see me as assertive. I think it's important for people to see that women can have different leadership styles.

My volunteer work has mainly been around women and education. As part of the MIT Alumni Association in the Bay Area, I organized events for women's professional development. I even ran my daughters' Girls Scout Troop for about six years, which was super fun. Most recently, here at LAM, I started a mentoring program and affinity group for women.

Advice to Young Women

Success is transient. Tomorrow people will be saying, what's next? So I think it's all about having fun getting there. You really have to wake up in the morning wanting to do something. And you don't have to run after other people's idea of 'plum jobs'. Define your own 'plum job', great stuff that the organization is just not doing. That's where I've made my career.

It's also about where people have shone the spotlight in the past. The question is, can you redirect that spotlight?

AWARDS & HONOURS

- YWCA Golden Gate Silicon Valley Tribute to Women in Technology Award, 2021
- As part of the Soraa team, Light Fair Innovation Awards Finalist, 2017
- As part of the Soraa team, LEDs Magazine's Sapphire Award, 2016
- Two awarded patents for elements of equipment design, 2002 & 2005
- Numerous internal company awards for team excellence, 1998 – Present

ROAD LESS TRAVELLED

I made the choices which felt right, at each stage of my life.

Early Life

My father, Prof. M. S. Vardya, was a scientist at the Tata Institute of Fundamental Research. Like all the other kids on the campus, I gravitated towards science, it was just the done thing. My elder brother and several cousins were from various IITs.To give JEE and do engineering seemed to be the best and most logical thing to do. So, I worked hard, got into IIT Bombay and took up Metallurgical Engineering.

Life at IIT Bombay

I went to a girl's school (J B Petit) till the 10th standard and then joined IIT where I was the only girl in my department, in a class of 40. It was a huge gender shock for me but things settled down after some time and I felt comfortable. Of course, being the only girl in class had its privileges! Receiving the Institute Silver Medal for standing first in my department was the high point of my academic life. Surviving in a male-dominated environment of IIT Bombay helped me when I joined the corporate world. Though I am an introvert, I never hesitate to speak up.

The high point of my personal life at IIT was meeting my husband, Rizwan. He was in the Electrical Engineering department, I had heard of him but never really interacted. One Friday evening, on my way home, I met him at the Vikhroli station ticket counter. We travelled back together and that was the beginning of a long lasting friendship and our life journey together. I guess that's what we call destiny!

REKHA KOITA
B.Tech, Metallurgical Engineering and Materials Science, 1992

Co-founder, Koita Foundation
President, CMU Mumbai Alumni Network

"Be confident of yourself, of your work, of what you're doing."

Time has flown !

Ours was an inter-religious marriage, not very common in India even today. To allay the fears and hesitation of our families is a topic which needs a book by itself! But all's well that ends well and what remains with us is the final outcome – a lifetime of close-knit relations.

Professional Journey

From IIT, I went on to do my Masters in Materials Science from Carnegie Mellon University. I returned to India after graduation, as part of my original plan, a rarity in those days. But there were no jobs in my area of specialisation - thin film semicon-

DSA Award Function, 2019

ductors. I decided to change gears and joined Andersen Consulting (now Accenture). Joining consulting was serendipity but I am glad I made the switch. I was a management consultant for the next 8 years and enjoyed it thoroughly. My work focussed on business process optimization and technology.

My most precious people !

Shifting Gears

In 2003, I decided to take a personal break for a couple of years as I had small children and aging parents to take care of, which was hard to do alongside a consulting career. When I got back in 2006, I worked in the social sector, along with doing corporate training in consulting skills. In 2016, Rizwan and I set up Koita Foundation, with the objective of helping NGOs in digital transformation initiatives, using technology and data analytics to enhance their productivity, impact and scale.

> **IIT BOMBAY, TO ME IS: HOME AND HOMECOMING.**

We have had very good success as NGOs were finding it extremely challenging to get support for technology and capacity building. Support also involved providing guidance and hand holding them through the journey. Digital transformation for NGOs has been successful for us as it aligns needs of NGOs with our skills. My decision to join the social sector reminds me of Ludwig Wittgenstein's quote – "How small a thought it takes to fill someone's life".

At around the same time, I also got involved with the Silver Jubilee Reunion (SJRU) activities of our batch, as one of the Legacy Project leaders. I took up the LP initiatives thinking that it would be a good opportunity to do something interesting, but never realised the impact it would have on me. After graduating in 1992, I had kept in touch with a handful of friends and rarely visited IITB campus. I have now reconnected with more than 200 batchmates and made so many new friends – perhaps more than I made in 4 years at IITB. I started going to campus regularly and interacting with a range of faculty, administrators and students – which has been an amazing experience where I have learned a lot and grown tremendously.

I have been driving the implementation of several projects – Bandhu (enhancing the emotional well being of students), creating travel grants for UG students, setting up Cafe 92 - which is perhaps the most trending place on IITB campus now! All in all, it has been an extremely gratifying experience and has had a delightful influence on my life.

Based on my experience at IITB, I started engaging actively with the CMU Alumni network after a break of over 20 years. I am the President of CMU Mumbai Alumni Network for the past 5 years.

A Lasting Legacy

In 2021, Rizwan and I supported IIT Bombay in establishing the Koita Center for Digital Health (KCDH), an inter-disciplinary center. It is the first of its kind in India, focused on driving academic programs, research, and industry collaborations and entrepreneurship in Digital Health – a sunrise sector. KCDH offers a minor program, dual degree and PhD programs in digital health informatics. The coursework includes computer science, statistics, mathematics, as well as public health, epidemiology and biology. We have faculty from leading hospitals across India including Tata Memorial Hospital and AIIMS Delhi. We are grateful to IITB for giving us the opportunity to collaborate closely with fac-

H10 gang after 25 years !

RAPID FIRE

I believe: In doing my best in whatever I take up. Give it time.
I love: Having quiet time to myself, especially in the morning.
The world needs: A lot of empathy and a lot of love.
I'm passionate about: Working in the field of education and mental health.
I wish: I had kind of been a little less hard on myself when I was younger.
Success is: being at peace with yourself.
The most important thing to remember when I step into work: Keeping my goals for the day.

ulty and administration in developing the centre.

Work-Life Balance

At every stage, it was about really thinking through what are my priorities; what's going to be good, not just for me, but for the overall ecosystem (i.e. the family). Interestingly, Rizwan left his job to become an entre-

Workshop at IIT B

At Café 92 on Campus with my batchmates

preneur one month after we got married! He has been really busy since then with a lot of travel. There were many responsibilities – with aging parents and young kids. I believed there was a lot of potential in what Rizwan was trying to do, and I supported his dream. I adjusted my work where needed, and really enjoyed my time with my kids, my in-laws and parents. I look back with a lot of fulfilment and no regrets.

My boys have grown up now - Samad just graduated from IIT Bombay (Computer Science) and Sahil will be joining an undergraduate program in Economics. I have now moved to near fulltime work at Koita Foundation.

Advice to Young Women

Be confident of yourself, of your work, of what you're doing. Speak up and make the choices that are okay for you. Also decide, where is it that you want to spend your time and energy? Don't fight over small stuff. Just let it go and focus on your main goals.

AWARDS & HONORS

- Recipient, Distinguished Service Award, IIT Bombay.
- Institute Silver Medal, IIT Bombay.

CLIMB EVERY MOUNTAIN

The idea of diversity is that nobody wants to be treated as ABCD, you want to be an equal.

Early Life

I come from a typical Army family background. My dad got transferred every couple of years, so my siblings and I grew up in small towns like Ambala, Secunderabad, Bangalore (it was small back then!) and Jabalpur. We went to local schools, had friends from different parts of the country. We never identified ourselves as Tamilian, or South Indian, we were Indian.

My dad lost his father when he was three years old. So, he was pretty much a self-made man. He wanted to see his boys and girls well educated. In Tambrahm families they say, either you study well, or you will be herding the cows. In the case of girls, you would be married off early. So all that sort of pushed us to make something of ourselves.

I have two elder brothers, one was doing postgraduation in science, the other went into engineering. When I finished my schooling, I was packed off to Madras to be with my maternal grandparents. I started preparing for the entrance exam, side by side. It was just good luck that I got into IIT, because I got rejected by all the local colleges!

I actually joined the M.Sc. Physics program. But there were just 12 students in the class, including the AIR JEE rank 1. And though I loved physics, I really felt out of their league. I also realized I didn't want to be an academic or researcher, I wanted to be more real and do something with my hands. So, in the second year, I switched to electrical engineering.

Life at IIT Bombay

I went in at 16 and came out at 21 - those five years transformed me

REVATHI KASTURI

B.Tech, Electrical Engineering, 1980

Founder & CEO, LAQSH Job Skills Academy

"There's no beautiful formula for work-life balance."

Proud family with mom, daughter Anandhi and her husband Varadarajan at her graduation at INSEAD Fontainbleau

Reaching for the skies

completely. There were so many clubs, from hiking to foreign films, music, sports, you name it. I dabbled in a little bit of everything, exploring so many things I didn't have access to before. I was like a sponge, picking up a little bit from everybody and everything around me.

The seniors in the hostel were more like elder sisters and moms, you could confide in them, and they would say, "Don't worry, you will settle in, you will shine". I found my identity as a person, as a woman on campus. I understood something about social issues, and how important they were for me. It was also my first brush with feminism.

> **IIT BOMBAY, TO ME IS: WHERE I MET KINDRED SPIRITS AND DISCOVERED MY VOICE.**

We lived in what was then called the 'Ladies Hostel' and that label irked all of us. So one fine night, a few of us took a bicycle, a can of paint and changed all the signboards on campus from 'Ladies Hostel' to H10. The next day, we sent a letter to the administration saying that henceforth, we are to be addressed as H10.

There were archaic rules, such as curfew after 8 pm, only for girls. A few of us made it a point to climb down the pipes, go fetch samosas and lassis and come back after 8 pm. That was our way of registering a protest, saying 'this is not fair'. At the general body meeting we managed to convince everybody that the girls hostel should allow visitors, just like the boys hostel did.

I learnt that if you want to do something, you have to be assertive and work hard for it.

When I was told 'girls are not allowed on hikes' I marched into the Diro's house, which was right across from H10 and said, "Sir, we want to go on this hike". He (Prof. A.K. De) listened to us and said, "Okay, no problem. But I'll get a professor to chaperone you". So Prof. Rehana Ghadially sportingly came along. It was exhilarating but poor Prof. Rehana was not the trekking type. It was very difficult for her; the boys literally had to carry her while coming back.

But she gave a clean sheet to the Diro

and, said, "These kids are all fine, just let them go".

Professional Journey

I joined Tata Burroughs straight from campus, without putting much thought into it. Software was a new field back then so great opportunities, a lot of learning and a lot of travel.

Then I moved to Wipro because I wanted to be based in India. Wipro was a hardware company but also provided services to build applications ground up, like payroll, ERP etc to its clients.

But when readymade software packages became available, they no longer needed an army of coders. So I

On top of the world with my daughter

got into field engineering services and went on to head sales for one region, then two regions and then the entire country. I enjoyed the transition from being a technical person to a supervisory role and then actually taking responsibility for business and leadership.

After handling the domestic business for a couple of years, I went into the international business and headed the finance vertical for Wipro. Excellent journey of 17 years, then I started Tarang Software with a couple of my colleagues.

Again, heady days, we had VCs approaching us and saying, "Hey, you guys, here's the money, please start your business". But then 9/11 happened and all our business plans went for a huge toss. The telecom industry in Europe collapsed, US was in chaos, we had to rethink. I think IIT Bombay taught you resilience, how to pick yourself up each time. We went through various ups and downs before it finally got established. I sold my stake to the investors and decided to do something in the social space.

Giving Back

In 2008, I started Laqsh Job Skills Academy. What youth want is the skills and the education to be able to access a job, and to have a good life. So we work with government schools across the country to impart skills in electronics, IT, finance,

In the lap of nature

beauty and wellness. The idea is to make the youth employable or even start their own entrepreneurial ventures.

It is a for-profit venture in order to be sustainable but the primary focus is social impact. We believe that skills must be integrated with academics. Skill training is for everyone, not just dropouts. With my background in technology, I wanted to build online content and Learning Management Systems but every time I went to the government, they would politely hear me out and do nothing.

Then came the pandemic, schools closed overnight and everything changed. We started by training all our 500 odd trainers across the country in how to use screens and be comfortable with new technology for teaching. During the peak of the lockdown, we had 30,000 students in class everyday.

Another cause which is close to my heart is bringing greater gender diversity into boardrooms and C-suites. I am part of the Diversify Club which aims to see that more and more women get a seat on corporate boards. And for that purpose, we provide training and support, creating a pipeline of eligible candidates.

Work-Life Balance

There's no beautiful formula for this great work life balance. Everybody is different and we all manage. I'm a single mom supported completely by my parents. They were always at home when my daughter was growing up. For me, it was always work first and then life and family fitted around that. It was understood that you had to make choices.

I remember, when she was in 5th or 6th class, one day my daughter came home and said we had a debate in school about working moms vs stay-at-home. You know how it is with all of us women who are working, there is this deep sense of guilt. So I almost stopped breathing and I was waiting and she says, "Don't worry. The working mom side won".

The kids concluded that stay-at-home moms are helicopter parents while working moms are the 'cool' type. Hearing that was such a relief!

Advice to Young Women

I took the plunge into the social space when I felt I had built a decent kitty, taken care of my child to go to college etc. But if you are committed and feel passion for a cause, you needn't wait.

NGOs nowadays pay you enough to enjoy a decent quality of life. I would also like to see IIT students mentor kids from tier 2, tier 3 towns and inspire them to pursue their dreams.

RAPID FIRE

I believe: That we can all make a positive difference to the world.
I love: hiking and nature.
The world needs: people who can stand up and be counted.
The stuff I don't sweat: Money
Success is: Good night's sleep. Feeling like you have lived life well.
One thing I wish somebody had told me when I was 18: Be proud of who you are instead of wanting to 'fit in'.

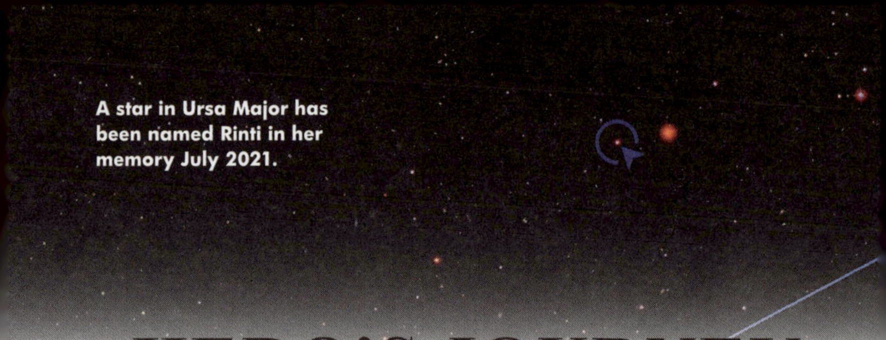

HERO'S JOURNEY

She came into this world early, she left this world early, but she left it a better place.

Early Life

Doctors gave Rinti a 1% chance of survival at birth. Her mother was hospitalised for surgery in the 26th week of pregnancy, when Rinti decided she could wait no longer and arrived in this world. For several weeks she fought hard for survival in the neonatal Intensive Care Unit and triumphed.

She grew up in Mumbai in a typical Bengali family which greatly valued education. Rinti's father was an eminent economist while her mother held a PhD in addition to being a homemaker. A class topper and National Talent Scholar, Rinti set very high standards for herself.

One day, she returned from school crying profusely after results were announced. Her parents got worried and wondered whether she had failed in one of the subjects. Her brother, who was studying in the same school, informed smilingly that Rinti was crying because she had scored 98% and not 100% in one of the subjects!

But Rinti was not just focused on marks. The outside-the-box thinking, which was to become her hallmark, was kindled in her school days by Mrs Vasanta Subramanian, a teacher at Mumbai's Cathedral and John Connon School. "Her methods and ideas were my first exposure to innovative thinking," Rinti had posted in a Facebook tribute to Mrs Subramanian in 2013.

With two elder brothers doing their B.Tech. at IIT Bombay, Rinti chose to follow in the footsteps of her

DR. RINTI BANERJEE

PhD, Biomedical Engineering, 2000

Madhuri Sinha Chair PROFESSOR at the Department of Biosciences & Bioengineering at IIT Bombay

Staycation with son Pulak to celebrate husband's birthday, Mumbai, India, October 11, 2019

grandfather, a doctor. So, although she qualified for both engineering and medicine after 12th, Rinti chose to pursue MBBS at B. J. Medical College, Pune.

Life as a Medico

One of Rinti's MBBS classmates recalls Rinti being brilliant at diagnosing patients. "Classmates used to approach Rinti for their doubts and she was always kind to students who needed help. She never displayed a sense of superiority." And Rinti extended the same kindness to her patients.

"In second year of MBBS, Rinti was late to a class… She had spent the morning standing in queue to purchase medicines for a young cardiac patient. On the previous day, she had learnt that the patient did not have money to buy medicines. Rinti took money from her father for the treatment, without telling him the reason. The patient recovered and returned a month later, specifically to thank Rinti, even though she was not a qualified doctor."

Another MBBS classmate remembers Rinti as a very cheerful, lively, talkative person. "We always used to sit nearby for our lectures and clinical tutorials. I remember during our 2nd year [MBBS], Rinti was absent for a few days. She suddenly turned quiet and withdrawn and was not talking to anyone. We tried to talk

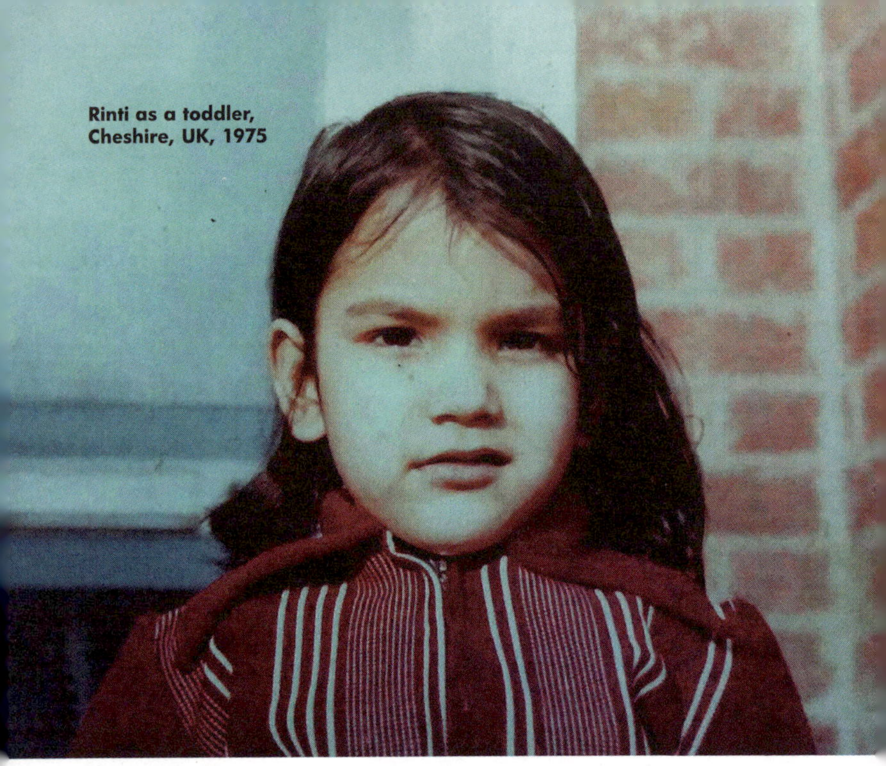

Rinti as a toddler, Cheshire, UK, 1975

to her but without success. A week later, she revealed that there was a miscarriage [in the family] and she was upset and shaken because of that. She cried a lot that day."

This sensitive nature was put to the test when she went to Rajasthan to pursue MD in General Medicine. Having grown up in Mumbai and Pune, Rinti found that people in Rajasthan were orthodox, especially in their treatment towards women. As a doctor, she saw cases of abused and suppressed women in her wards.

As a professional too, she felt that her male colleagues did not respect her abilities as an equal because she was a woman. After about 2 months, she just left Rajasthan and came home to Pune, without informing her parents or anyone else, about her decision to quit MD. That was the beginning of Rinti's journey outside clinical practice.

> "
>
> **A HEARTFELT TRIBUTE TO A BRILLIANT INNOVATOR AND TEACHER, LOVING MOTHER, DAUGHTER, WIFE, AUNT AND ALL-ROUND INSPIRING HUMAN BEING.**

Non-medico Journey

Working in the clinical setting during MD had made Rinti realize, that in a hospital, she would not be able to do any research or develop innovative products. So, she decided to pursue PhD at IIT Bombay in the school of biomedical engineering on development of novel lung surfactants, a topic that was dear to her heart.

Being born pre-term, Rinti was determined to improve chances of survival of pre-term babies. Lack of lung surfactants in pre-term babies was a known, leading cause of mortality and Rinti developed novel lung surfactants during her PhD. She completed her work in a record time of 2.5 years. She continued to research on lung surfactants for the first 15 years of her career and published more than 30 research papers and filed several patents.

Rinti joined IIT Bombay as one of the youngest faculty members in 2001. She got promoted to Associate Professor in 2005 and Professor in 2009. But her journey as a medico in a technology institute was not easy. Her family says, "Very few people understood her unique strengths of being a translational researcher with a medical degree in a technology institute. She did not fit the compartmentalized definition of a traditional engineer or doctor and many failed to see that she was both."

As an innovator, Rinti wanted the benefits of her work to reach the masses and worked hard for inclusive healthcare. And here lay the real challenge. To commercialise lung surfactants, a pharma company would need to conduct clinical trials which could cost up to US$1 billion and no company was ready to invest in trials of innovative products. Most of her initial innovations never reached the commercial stage due to lack of such investment in clinical trials.

Disheartened, she shifted focus to applying her technologies from drug delivery to other domains like nutraceuticals and smart materials, which had shorter regulatory cycles. Delivering nutrition through cosmetics (henna, bindi, lipstick, multani mitti, moisturizer, skin lotion etc) became one of her new passions.

Her idea was to reduce non-compliance to medication in traditional formulations like tablets, capsules and syrups. Because her ideas were unconventional, often, the funding agencies did not support her work. Rinti had to seek out unconventional sources of funding. Bill and Melinda Gates Foundation (BMGF) gave her several grants to take some of her ideas forward.

In fact, in 2018 Rinti and her team won the BMGF Grand Challenges grant to develop a microneedle patch for contraceptive delivery. With a single application on the skin, the contraceptive would be effective for 6 months and eliminate the need of taking an oral contraceptive on a daily basis. The grant was given to only 3-4 other scientists in the world. Rinti's was one of the rare Indian labs which was well-staffed, well-funded and focused on commercialising its technologies.

Personal Life & Motherhood

When Rinti joined IIT Bombay for her PhD, her to-be husband was a fellow student. They did not interact much during her first year, as both

Memorial tree plantation at BSBE building, IIT Bombay, Mumbai, India, October 3, 2021

were introverts by nature. Being a medico, Rinti was not much familiar with computers and he helped out and both became friends later.

"She was intelligent, hardworking, focused, warm, emotionally intelligent, wonderful orator, ambitious, and beautiful!" Rinti's husband recalls fondly. "She made me a better person and she was my hero."

After her unpleasant stint in Rajasthan during MD, Rinti never imagined that she would one day be comfortable to marry her husband who is from Rajasthan.

A transformative point for Rinti was the birth of her son Pulak in March 2007. She did not slow down during her pregnancy. She worked until the 9th month of pregnancy and resumed work 6 months after her son's birth.

In fact, Rinti published 26 research papers between 2007 to 2009. Additionally, in 2008, she was felicitated by the Society for Cancer Research and Communication for research achievements. "Rinti balanced work and personal life extremely well," says her husband. "Rinti was very close to her parents and Pulak."

Rinti and Pulak had similar personalities and similar likings for food, weather, vacations, entertainment etc. Rinti's life revolved around her son. Like any other doting mother, she would pack his tiffin, water bottle, school bag, pick him up from school, and have lunch with him in the middle of her work-day. In the evening, she would help him with studies and projects regularly. She ensured that he was ahead in studies and never missed any of Pulak's extra-curricular events at school.

With family, Rinti often watched serials like Madam Secretary, Big Bang Theory, Young Sheldon, Grey's Anatomy, Friends, Castle, Suits, and Bones. She liked playing cards and board games like Sorry, Sequence, Apples to Apples, Scrabble, Monopoly and carrom. Listening to pop songs by Enrique Iglesias, Bono, Richard Marx, Backstreet Boys, One Direction, Ed Sheeran and watching SRK movies were stress busters for her.

In her spare time, she watched TED

talks and YouTube videos by prominent scientists. Despite her numerous degrees and vast experience, Rinti spent a lot of time learning on online platforms. She was certified in areas of global health, social entrepreneurship, intellectual property law and business strategies for social impact.

(un) Finished Dreams and Hurried Departure

Rinti was probably the only person in her department who did not take coffee/tea breaks. She nearly had double the output in half the lifetime. During Covid lockdown, she was all the more energized and came up with numerous Covid-relevant innovations.

Among them are, Duraprot wash resistant antiviral coated masks, Duraprot plus coated N95 masks (free of plastics) and alcohol free, natural ingredient derived, childsafe, skin-friendly disinfectant sprays. She also developed an immunity boosting nutraceutical drink.

Rinti's technologies had been licensed to 26 companies/ organizations. Few were not commercialized even after technology transfer. Hence, she decided to start her own company, which would give her complete freedom to commercialize any product she wanted.

PicoVie Innovations LLP was registered in the third week of May 2021. A week later, Rinti was hospitalized after contracting Covid. She was admitted to the Intensive Care Unit for the second time in her life. As earlier, for 6 week s she fought very hard for survival but this time she succumbed to post-Covid complications.

Deeply mourned by her family, friends, colleagues and students, Rinti Banerjee led a bold and brilliant life - she arrived in this world early and departed from this world early.

Her life continues to inspire others and her journey towards inclusive healthcare continues through her students, alumni and family.

Prepared from inputs of Bhagwati Prasad, Rinti's husband.

AWARDS & HONORS WHICH WERE DEAR TO RINTI

1. Young Researcher Grant Award, International Foundation for Science, Sweden 2004.
2. National Award for Women Bioscientists, under 45 category, by Department of Biotechnology, Govt of India in 2012.
3. H H Mathur Award for Excellence in Research in Applied Sciences 2016 - 17 from IIT Bombay.
4. Elected Fellow of Indian Academy of Science, Bangalore and Fellow of National Academy of Sciences, India.
5. Excellence in teaching award for the year 2018 - 2019.
6. Advising Editor of ACS Omega and Associate Editor of ACS Biomaterials Science and Engineering: ACS (American Chemical Society journals are highly reputed).
7. Published > 200 research papers and filed more than 40 patents.
8. Becoming TEDx speaker, 2018

"Choose a problem that excites you and not just what's in fashion."

ALL THAT MATTERS

In science, you also need to be lucky to hit upon an interesting problem.

Early Life

I grew up in a middle class household in Pune. My father studied politics and economics upto B.A. but had to discontinue his studies, despite winning a scholarship, due to financial constraints. My mother studied upto 2nd year of college but despite being first in Sanskrit and winning a scholarship at BHU, she got married due to social constraints.

My mother finished her B.A. and M.A. after we four sisters were born. As you can see, education was a very important aspect of life in my family and we were all encouraged to excel.

The seeds of my life in science were sown when I decided to appear for the 'State Scholarship Examination' which used to be conducted in 7th grade. The examination had a paper in 'General Science'. Since my venerable and highly reputed girls' school taught only 'Home Science' till the 7th grade, it was not a surprise that no student from my school had gotten this scholarship.

My teachers agreed to teach me outside the school hours and on holidays. My math teacher (Mrs. Sowani) asked me to come to her house as her husband (Bhau Sowani) was known to be an excellent science teacher. Not only did he teach me things that I needed to know to succeed in the examination but he opened my eyes to the world of science in general.

He pointed me to a popular science magazine called 'Srishti Dnyan' in Marathi, nurtured my interest in mathematics and encouraged me to participate in science essay competitions. Incidentally, I did get the scholarship (only 10 were given). I was mighty proud as the amount was just 1 INR less than my school fee.

After my B.Sc. from Pune University, I applied to IIT Bombay and IIT

PADMA SHRI DR. ROHINI GODBOLE

MSc. IIT Bombay, 1974. (silver medallist)

Honorary Professor, Center for High Energy Physics, Indian Institute of Science Bangalore.

Receiving D.Sc. at IITK in December 2021

In the office at IISc, when I moved there in 1995

Kanpur. IIT Kanpur was rated a little higher for physics at that time, so I wanted to go there. But my parents said, look, if you fall ill, we can come to Bombay in 4 hours. If you are in Kanpur, it will take us 19 hours. So that's why I opted for IIT Bombay.

I must add that I was able to join IIT only because of the National Science Talent Scholarship, of Rs 200 or 250 per month (a princely sum at the time!). My father would not have been able to spend that much money on me, in spite of the fact that he was a high ranking government officer, I had three siblings and salaries back then were modest indeed!

Life at IIT Bombay

Coming from a Marathi medium college in Pune I was worried about fitting in. How will I speak in English? This was a far bigger insecurity in me than being a woman in STEM. There was also a marked difference between the way a subject was taught in IIT vs the university. Quizzes, home assignments, open book exams - these were all new to me.

> **"IIT BOMBAY, TO ME IS: A PLACE WHERE MY JOURNEY INTO THE UNKNOWN BEGAN.**

With two dear friends from IITB LH, taken as a memory while leaving the institute for new abodes

The B.Tech. girls in the hostel (called LH: the Ladies Hostel) were also not much help as they continuously wondered whether our 'fundas were gol (zero)'! I dare say this impression changed reasonably quickly. We had our share of fun as well. Lakeside walks, Sahyadri treks, listening to songs in the night at Mood Indigo,

Stop by a lakeside while driving to the Olympic Games in Montreal in 1976

seeing Hindi and English films in the Convo…

Intellectually, the atmosphere was great and so were some of the teachers. Professor S. H. Patil in particular has been a big influence. If I'm a theoretical physicist today, it is because of the 'home paper' that I did with him which made me see the beauty in the subject. I had to work quite hard to reach up to his standards.

We were a class of 17, just 3 girls, but we never ever faced any hostility or any bad treatment from our classmates. To be frank, gender was simply never an issue which affected our interactions. I have checked with my classmates (both male and female) and they agree with me. So this is not a fanciful reconstruction.

Most of the teachers did not discriminate either, at least not in any obvious way. Though when I told Prof Patil that I want to go abroad to do a PhD he said, "Why do you want to go abroad?" Whereas to my junior he said, "Why stay in India, you should go outside". But when I said I have made up my mind, he wrote me a very good recommendation letter.

Professional Journey

I came back to India after my PhD in theoretical particle physics from Stonybrook University. If you look at it professionally, it was not a great decision. I should have done a post-doctoral fellowship after my PhD as I had offers in Europe and USA. But at that time I just wanted to be home. So I joined the Tata Institute of Fundamental Research as a post doctoral fellow (PDF).

I published three papers in a journal called Physical Review Letters in the early days I spent in TIFR (it was like getting a paper in Nature, for physics). I was in my late 20s at the time. Post-TIFR, I worked briefly at the Royal Institute of Science (Mumbai) and then joined the University of Bombay as a lecturer.

Even after joining the University of Bombay, I was very lucky to continue my collaborations with some senior collaborators at TIFR with whom wavelengths matched and also with the younger postdoctoral fellows and PhD students. There was no official MOU between the University of Bombay and TIFR but a

Prof. S.H. Patil around his 65th birthday, surrounded by generations of his students !

true collaboration doesn't need these formal things.

New Horizons in Physics

With the discovery of the Higgs Boson in 2012, physicists have a complete picture of all the fundamental particles that we know of. But at the same time, there is 'dark matter' for which we have no explanation. The other puzzle is the dominance of matter over anti-matter. So clearly, there is physics beyond the world of standard model, which is known as 'BSM' physics.

One such model which I had worked on is called Supersymmetry. But the same Large Hadron Collider experiments which gave us the evidence for the Higgs have not given any evidence for the particles predicted in these models. So now we are also looking at cosmic microwave background radiation in the universe or light/ neutrinos/ gravitational waves coming from the stars and galaxies for answers.

To make progress on this path we need experts in machine learning to handle the big data, theorists who explore the mysteries of gravitation, experimentalists who probe the universe and cosmos through multiwavelength astronomy. This is the decade of astroparticle physics.

RAPID FIRE

If I could, I would: Remove discrimination and ensure that the world is a fair place.
I love: Nature.
I'm passionate about: Particle physics, and women in science
I wish: That we all get to live the life we want. And not what somebody else chooses for us.
The stuff I don't sweat: Politics.
The most important thing to remember when I step into work: Today is a new day.

Work-Life Balance

Apart from research, during the early days in Mumbai I used to teach women in a slum to read and write and I was also part of a group against nuclear weapons. I was not particularly interested in 'settling down'. Luckily, my parents really supported me. Then I got the chance to go to Germany for a post-doctoral position. There, I met a German particle physicist Dr Marek Nowakowski and we got married.

For 6-8 years, I was in India while he was in Europe. I would travel to Europe in summer, he came to India at Christmas time. I must say that was perhaps one of the toughest time in my life but also perhaps the most exciting. I had chosen to do this, so I didn't feel the pressure. I did some of my most important work in this period.

I constructed my own support bridges - like-minded friends and people who shared my passion. The only seriously negative part in this whole journey was that we postponed having children. And somehow, we didn't have them. But I have nephews and nieces who I am very close to. And young students give me all the affection and the love I need. Dr Nowakowski and I had a beautiful partnership but at some point, we drifted apart. We are no longer married.

Women in Science

The first international conference on Women in Physics was organized by International Union of Pure and Applied Physics in the year 2001. I was invited to speak about my experience as a woman physicist in India who had achieved some measure of success, and it resonated with the audience.

Women from Ghana, Mauritius, Egypt came to me and said that when Western women talk, we feel that they are from a different culture. But when we listen to you, we feel - 'if she can do it, we can do it too!'. This made me think that if we can share the stories of more women scientists from India, it can inspire young girls to be future scientists of India.

So with Prof. Ram Ramaswamy I started a project on behalf of the Indian Academy of Sciences and its panel for 'Women in Science' of which I was the founding chair. We approached 200 women scientists and finally, 99 stories were published in a book called 'Lilavati's Daughters'. The title is a tribute to Lilavati, a female mathematician in ancient India, as per folklore.

Since that time I have been working in a lot of fora to increase the participation of women in science and make it more effective.

Advice to Young Women

Follow your dream. Choose a problem that excites you and not just what's in fashion.

HONORS & AWARDS

- Padma Shri (2019).
- Distinguished Alumna of IIT Bombay (2004).
- DSC from the Indian Institute of Technology in Kanpur (2021).
- Ordre National du Mérite by the French government (2021).

Among the few women who have been elected to all the three academies of Science in India and The World Academy of Sciences for physical sciences.

"It's not how many times you fall down, it's how many times you get up."

Roopa reading at Book Passage

DISCOVERY DIVA

I felt a real sense of purpose that I'm making a difference for people who are marginalized.

Early Life

I grew up mostly in Mumbai. My father, who was in the IAS and had a Math/ Statistics education, inspired me both with a love of learning and hard work. My mother was more into being compassionate, being caring for others. So it was a really good balance.

We always had a lot of books at home including popular science books, fiction, and biographies. That was the one thing my father always indulged in. My brother is nine years younger and much smarter than me (he stood second all India in the IIT JEE in his year). Most of the things he'd ask, I would say, I don't know. So that pushed me to find out, for example, 'why is the sky blue'?

I was a good student and got selected as a National Talent Search Exam scholar. But I didn't have a clear idea of what to pursue as a career. I remember, just after my 10th grade, I was sitting on the lawn having snacks with my classmate Johara Shahabuddin. She mentioned that her brother was in IIT and that she would like to study there too. So I was like - "Oh, maybe I can go to IIT too".

Also, I hated frog dissection so I knew I had no future in medicine. Engineering was a better bet but I almost didn't give JEE, thinking it's too tough. Dad persuaded me. "What's the worst that can happen?", he said. My JEE rank was 594 so I just missed the cut-off for Engineering Physics. However, Professor Kudchadkar convinced my father and me to go for ChemE.

Life at IIT Bombay

285 guys and 14 girls - that was my batch at IITB. That can be overwhelming, right? In class, when

DR. ROOPA RAMAMOORTHI

B.Tech, Chemical Engineering, 1989

Senior Associate Director for the Catalyst Program and Innovation Ventures (InVent) Philanthropy Fund at University of California, San Francisco

With the Catalyst team and Catalyst interns.

you are one of only three girls, you hesitate to ask a question. What if it's a dumb question? People will remember. So I would instead go after class and speak to the professor. It's a habit that's stuck with me till today when I prefer approaching a speaker after the talk.

> **IIT BOMBAY, TO ME IS: THE OPPORTUNITY TO EXCEL AND FORM CLOSE FRIENDSHIPS.**

In my first year, honestly, I was involved in too many activities. I acted in three plays, took part in basketball and what not. So my GPA was only 7.1. In the second year, I was like, I really need to focus and my GPA jumped to 9.0. I did not give up on extracurricular activities but balanced it out, away from semester crunch time.

I remember in Physics-1, I got nervous during the exam and got an E. I had to retake the exam to get a D. But then I managed a 990 in AGRE engineering which was the highest score in my year among non-CS people who do not take AGRE engineering. That gave me a lot of confidence, that I can compete with anyone. Later, I got 2340 in GRE, second highest in my batch. I also stood second in my ChemE class at IITB.

Other high points at IITB were the lifelong friendships developed in H10. And taking part in two 'Himankans'. I went on two wonderful Himalayan treks, one to the Garhwal region and the other one to Kashmir. And in my final year, I organised the first-ever Aqua Games at Mood Indigo.

Professional Journey

Initially, I thought I wanted to be a professor and so I decided to pursue a PhD. Being second in my class with my strong GRE and AGRE scores I got into all the top universities, including Stanford, MIT, University of Wisconsin, Princeton, Carnegie Mellon, and Caltech, with full fellowships or graduate research assistantships.

I chose Caltech due to an eminent professor in biochemical engineering being there. Also, coming from India, the warm weather was attractive. While being a strong school with many Nobel laureates, Caltech is also a small school, where I thought I would feel more at home. However, in those days Caltech had a very poor ratio of women to men in the undergrad and graduate programs.

My PhD in biochemical engineering at Caltech was challenging because my advisor moved to Switzerland after three years. I had to find a new advisor and switch my topic. So, effectively, after doing that, I finished my thesis in just two years. Then I did a couple of postdocs, one at University of Washington and another at MIT. The hardest part at MIT was getting used to the Boston winters!

Initially, I wanted to be a professor. But then I came to Berkeley because my husband was there and I went into pharma. I worked with Bayer, where I got exposed to how one really develops products. I was part of a three-woman team that did the viral validation work for a protein therapeutic that went into clinical trials.

ChemE class photo

With the basketball team at Inter-IIT in Delhi

After I went through a difficult divorce, I was looking for work that was meaningful. As Associate Director for partnering and scientific affairs at Bio Ventures for Global Health, I put together collaborations between leading academic universities, nonprofits and pharmaceutical companies to accelerate the development of drugs, vaccines and diagnostics for neglected tropical diseases like TB and malaria. I actually put together more than 90 collaborations, some of which are advancing. I felt a real sense of purpose that I'm making a difference for people who are marginalized. I not only interacted with leading scientists in the pharma sector, whether at AstraZeneca, GSK, Sanofi, Novartis, but also with researchers from Cameroon, Nigeria, Kenya, India, China, Brazil, etc. So it was really being part of a global community that was very enriching.

RAPID FIRE

I believe: Integrity is important.
I love: Seeing others succeed and in a small way, if I've been part of their journey.
The world needs: Compassion and caring and being there to support each other.
I wish: To see more women and underrepresented minorities in STEM at the highest levels.
Success is: Feeling content, knowing you have done your best and it's a journey.
One thing I wish somebody had told me when I was 18: Life can get messy. Build your support structure for the hard times.

Being a Catalyst

What I do now is help UCSF faculty move discoveries forward, whether it's therapeutics, medical devices, diagnostics, digital health or bio tools. I am managing the therapeutics and medical device tracks at the UCSF Catalyst program. The goal is to allow a longer incubation period for projects within UCSF, so they get greater value both for the investigators as well as the university when they are spun out into Venture Capital backed companies or licensed out. I work with the principal investigators and understand what are the bottlenecks. So it's a lot of combining project management - delving into the science, looking at new ideas and how they can be translated towards products, and getting projects to apply for the Catalyst program and the Invent fund. It's wonderful when they actually reach milestones and are able to be spun out or licensed.

It's also very satisfying to run the Catalyst Internship program. We've had over 200 Catalyst interns - grad students and postdocs, clinical fellows and residents, who get the opportunity to learn about what is involved in bringing products from the bench to the bedside.

At Catalyst, I think of myself as an enabler, facilitating faculty members to advance their projects on the translational path. For example Prof. Hani Goodarzi got seed funding of 100k from Catalyst, which helped with critical experiments. His company Exai Bio just raised $67 million in a Series A to take forward a liquid biopsy platform that is focused on early detection of cancer.

Another of my favorites - Prof. Julie Saba - she's working on an ultra rare disease. It's not a project that can go the venture capital route but she got a small grant from the Catalyst program. Now she's getting $1.4 million from California Institute of Regenerative Medicine to do more of the preclinical work. That's one step closer to real world impact for patients.

Challenges as a Woman

At IIT, I remember there were some worker guys at the machine shop hitting on girls during the workshop. I couldn't go and work alone afterwards when I needed to do filing. A similar thing happened during my summer training at Hindustan Lever. At their factory in Andheri, there was a worker who was always drunk. My father had to ask for me to be transferred to the main office. These kind of things should have zero tolerance!

Work-Life Balance

Very honestly, I'm still struggling after my divorce. I think I relied on over-achieving as a way to deal with it. I did my PMP certification exam just two months after my separation. I was inspired by another IIT woman who went through a divorce. She ran a marathon, so surely I can do an exam, I thought at that time.

Soon after my separation, I wanted to do work that had a higher purpose and that is why I went into working in global health. I also started writing poetry - personal poems on topics like depression, anxiety, divorce and trying to rebuild my life - which has not been easy at all. It's a very vulnerable form of emotional communication which I share with the world. I was a finalist for the National Poetry Series in 2011. I've also performed at San Francisco Public Library. My poetry, essays and short stories, have been in over 70 publications, including a number of anthologies and on Perspectives on NPR and in India Currents.

Advice to Young Women

Girls in STEM, have confidence in yourself, even if people pull you down and say you can't do this or that. Be prepared to work hard and as the cliche goes, it's not how many times you fall down, it's how many times you get up.

AWARDS & HONORS

- Sherrie Wilkins Award for mentoring women from the Northern California chapters of AWIS (Association for Women In Science).

Sarita (bottom left) with Vikram (husband, IITB alum 1987), Anshul (son), and Aditi (daughter) (2018)

"Life is a marathon, not a sprint."

VIRTUAL WIZ

What excites me is that we are entering a new, immersive era of computing.

Early Life

Many women who wanted to apply to the IITs in the 80s could not because their families thought engineering wasn't for women, or did not want to send their daughters to live in hostels.

My parents also came from conservative backgrounds but never discriminated between my brother and me on the basis of gender. They were supportive of everything I did and always so proud of any successes I had. I was very fortunate to grow up in such an environment.

My mom was a school teacher/principal, then a homemaker, then a cooking teacher, and finally a bonsai artist and teacher. My dad is a paints and chemicals technologist. I attended Rev. C. F. Andrews School (up to 10th) and Jai Hind College for 11th and 12th. Since I liked Physics and Math, and did not like Biology, IIT seemed like the most appropriate option.

My parents valued hard work and my dad was a scientist at heart, they both inspired me throughout, to seek the best and do my best. I prepared for JEE by taking Agrawal classes. EE was a popular major that I could get into with my JEE rank, the little about EE we had in school I liked, so I signed up for it.

Life at IIT Bombay

There were just 11 women in my batch of 300+ students. Since we were such a small fraction, it could have been very isolating. But all the women lived in H10 and we had a very strong sense of community, even though our hostel was at the opposite end of the rest of campus life.

Most of the boys really didn't know how to talk to girls back then! Vikram was an exception – he was also in EE and we were lab partners. We hit it off and started seeing a lot of each other. The rest, as they say, is history.

As regards academics, my 3rd year

DR. SARITA ADVE

B.Tech, Electrical Engineering, 1987

Richard T. Cheng Professor of Computer Science at University of Illinois Urbana-Champaign

Sarita with her parents (Krishna Kumar and Santosh Arora), husband (Vikram Adve), and parents-in-law (Padmini and Sadanand Shetty), 2013

seminar and 4th year project both laid the foundation for the work I went on to do in my PhD. Prof. Rakesh Lal was my seminar advisor while Prof. Revankar was my B.Tech. project advisor. Both got me thinking about shared memory multiprocessors.

In the seminar I did a literature survey and then a project, along with two others from H-10 - Sujata and Tanuja. Three women on the same B.Tech. project was highly unusual and fortunate – 5 of us from our batch of 11 were in EE. We built a basic, shared memory multiprocessor for our project, using various off-the shelf parts. There is an iconic photograph of the three of us working on our PCB.

> **IIT BOMBAY, TO ME IS: THE PLACE THAT SHAPED MY PERSONAL AND PROFESSIONAL LIFE THE MOST.**

That's what I ended up doing for many years of my life after that (a more advanced version, but that was the starting point). So I'm forever grateful to my advisors and my teammates.

Prof. Vasi was also a huge influence. Both he and Prof. Lal would open up their lab, we could go and tinker around and build whatever we wanted to. I wish I had taken more advantage of it. But that spark of research and wanting to do something that one loves, I saw that in these professors. And that was something that stayed with me.

Professional Journey

I completed my PhD in Computer Science at the University of Wisconsin-Madison in 1993. After that, I joined Rice University as an assistant professor and then moved to Illinois in 1999. In my early work, with my PhD advisor, Mark Hill, I developed the idea of data-race-free memory consistency models for hardware and software.

Based on this work, with Hans Boehm, Bill Pugh, and others, I co-developed the memory models for the Java and C++ programming languages. This body of work forms the foundation of the semantics of shared memory for most hardware and software systems today.

My work has always been on the boundary of hardware and software. As another example, with my students and several collaborators, we developed software-driven solutions for dealing with hardware errors. Recently, Google announced that hardware errors have now become a big problem for their data centers and issued calls to action for solutions of the type we pioneered many years ago.

What excites me now is that we are entering a new, immersive era of computing. Similar to previous changes in computing modalities such as from mainframe to PCs to Web/ cloud-based to mobile, this new immersive era will also change how we build, program, and use computer systems. Immersive computing includes what we refer to as virtual, augmented, and mixed reality (collectively also referred to as extended reality or XR).

My group recently released ILLIXR (Illinois Extended Reality testbed), a fully open source XR system and launched the ILLIXR consortium to democratize XR systems research, development, and benchmarking.

Imagining the Future

Today virtual reality (VR) and augmented reality (AR) are largely used for gaming and entertainment but they have the potential to change pretty much everything we do. Surgeons are using VR and they want more realtime immersive technologies in the operating room. AR and VR can transform education, crisis response, retail services, and I am sure there are applications we haven't even imagined yet. On a more personal note, my dad lives in India and I would love to be able to have us interact with our holograms in our

Sarita, with her research group (2019)

Sarita with PhD advisor, Mark Hill, and his wife, Sue Dentinger (2016)

own living spaces, in realtime, with a seamless merge of the physical and the virtual, like we were right next to each other.

My research group is building the technologies for immersive systems that deliver on these promises. This requires interdisciplinary work spanning hardware, software, algorithms, and applications and is a long term research agenda for us.

RAPID FIRE

I believe: In living with integrity.
I'm passionate about: Work and life and balance and removing gender out of the equation.
If you fall: Be kind to yourself and move on
Success is: Influencing lasting positive change.
One thing I wish somebody had told me when I was 18: Develop a thick skin.

Challenges as a Woman

In 2010, I became a Fellow of the Association for Computing Machinery. A friend from IIT Bombay emailed me saying I was the first woman from India to get the recognition. That just blew my mind and changed my outlook in terms of gender issues.

Two of my colleagues did a study that quantified the number of women in the computer architecture community who had received awards or been invited to prestigious keynotes, panels, etc. The data showed that the recognition and participation of women was dismal.

This was a wake-up call for my community and yet, there was a subsequent highlight event with no invitations to women. This got many of us agitated and led to a major movement in our research community, with a clear call for a more diverse and inclusive environment.

During this time and also coinciding with the MeToo movement, a colleague wrote a blog quoting direct experiences of women facing discrimination and sexual harassment which shook people up. Although there were policies against such behavior, making a complaint was not easy and such incidents previously had not come to light.

We worked with our professional organization to institute a CARES committee consisting of trusted researchers who can be confidentially approached at a time of high vulnerability, and help navigate the process of filing complaints. The CARES movement has now taken off, many research communities have adopted it, and we received a distinguished service award from the Computing Research Association.

I recently co-founded and chair a similar Illinois CS CARES committee in my university department and the template is being scaled up for adoption in all college of engineering departments on my campus.

I want to add that I'm so proud of my H10 group. Three of us who joined H10 in 1983 - Sharada Srinivasan from my B.Tech. batch, Shobana Narasimhan from M.Sc. Physics, and I, were recently elected to the American Academy of Arts and Sciences. Others are in various successful roles in industry and academia. Each of us, in our own way, has managed multiple challenges, navigated the system and we hope to see many more women walk this path.

Work-Life Balance

Being a dual-career couple where both of us have pretty intense careers is not easy. My kids are awesome - I love them dearly - but the early years were pretty rough. Somehow, we hung in there. I have to acknowledge my husband, of course – we shared all household work - but also my parents and parents-in-law. They have all been absolutely incredible, cheering us all the way and being so supportive.

Now, as the kids have grown older, their care is slowly being replaced with the care of parents and old balls to juggle are being replaced with new ones. It is important to remember that life is a marathon and not a sprint. If one focuses too much on a single day, week, or even month or year, that proverbial balance between work and the rest of life may appear elusive.

But over the period of this marathon, I believe it is important - and certainly possible - to find that balance and do so in a way that is satisfying on all counts.

Advice to Young Women

This is such a fantastic time. So many women are leading the way as inspiring role models in so many different ways. We still need to see a lot of change, but we are getting there. In computer science, there's so much going on in terms of technical challenges, so much exciting work to do. We as technologists are building the future and, as women, we have the opportunity to shape this future for our needs, perhaps for the first time in such numbers and positions of power - isn't that exciting?

AWARDS & HONORS

- Sloan Foundation Research Fellowship (1998).
- ACM SIGARCH Maurice Wilkes Award, given to a mid-career researcher for an outstanding contribution to Computer Architecture (2008).
- Fellow of the Association for Computing Machinery (2010).
- Anita Borg Institute Women of Vision Award for Innovation (2012).
- ACM/IEEE-CS Ken Kennedy Award (2018).
- Elected to the American Academy of Arts and Sciences (2020).

THE STORYTELLER

It's the story that captivates, technology supports.

Early Life

I grew up in Bombay and I was very, very fascinated by Bollywood. I wanted to be part of the movie industry in some way. That was my dream. And when I was about 10 or 11, my dance troupe was invited to be part of a movie called 'Hum Bacche Hindustan Ke'. Sadly. when my parents took me to see it on the second day, it was gone from the theatre. Kind of tells you the calibre of that movie.

But that's what made me realise, hey, maybe acting or dancing is really not in my cards. I need to find another way to get into showbiz. The 'aha' moment came the first time I used a computer. I was a teenager and my father got a state of the art Silicon Graphics machine in his lab at TIFR. It was one of the only few machines in India at that time which could render graphics. As soon as I put my hands on it, I was hooked. My eyes just lit up and I knew that 'this was the future.' My father was a scientist, my mom was an artist. So computer graphics kind of combined those two forces in my head - the technical with the artistic.

SHALINI GOVIL PAI

B.Tech, Computer Science, 1990

VP & GM, TV@Google

"Keep experimenting."

I prepared for IIT with a very focused goal of doing computer science. To get into CS in IIT Bombay, you need a JEE rank below 100 but that didn't look impossible to me. I studied with the help of Agrawal classes (those were the gold standard back in the day). And I got a rank of 57 - don't know how, really - but it happened.

Life at IIT Bombay

IIT was an amazing experience - it changed the way I think about problems and gave me lifelong friendships. I fondly recall our midnight snack and cack sessions at the Chinese corner, which I think was called 'Rainbow'. My best friends are still from the IIT CS class. There are six of us at Google and we are each other's strongest supporters.

Being the only woman in class definitely meant that all the professors knew me, and if I was not in class, they knew I was not in class. But they were always really supportive. They took the time out to make sure that I was doing well and provide extra help when I needed it. I think they did realise it was harder for me.

The boys met at eleven in the night to do their homework in a group while I was solving problems all by myself. H10 was at one end of the campus and the boys' hostels were way off on the other side. But as I got into my junior and senior years I had such good friends in class, we were able to

Technical Director for the world's first entirely CG movie, Toy Story. With the heroes: Woody and Buzz

resolve this and did work together in groups from most projects.

I also met my husband, Raj, at IIT. We became friends in our senior year and kept in touch. He went to Hawaii while I was at Penn State. Then, it slowly started dawning on us that we probably like each other more than just friends. And so, that's where it went. And I'll say that Raj is my biggest supporter. Even if I doubt myself, he never doubts me.

Professional Journey

I had started to see a trend towards computers aiding movie making, as seen in movies like 'Star Wars' and early shorts like 'Tin Toy' from Pixar. Realizing that would get me to my dreams, I specialized in computer graphics at Penn State and then, I joined Pixar Animation, where I worked on 'Toy Story' and 'A Bug's Life'.

> **IIT BOMBAY, IS TO ME IS: MY TRAINING GROUND, MY ALMA MATER.**

I was very, very deep in the technology and in the rendering of our movies. Production life is pretty intense. We did 60 to 80 hours a week during production time. As a technical director, I articulated the variables that helped characters come to life.

Imagine assigning variables to the arm which say 'this is how you move the arm up and down'. Those variables were presented to the animators in a visual tool to make it happen in the frame.

After the animators did their job, we would add in texturing and lighting, making the whole scene very visually appealing and realistic.

We had a farm of Silicon Graphics machines that would render these scenes overnight. In the morning, we would all come in, sit together and comment on the motion. Is it popping? Is it not popping? Then we'd go back and redo it, if needed.

Just before launch, Disney had a focus group with kids and they were totally bored, even sleeping and yawning. We knew we had to redo it. It was a mad scramble because theatres were already booked. We redid a whole half hour of the film and in the end, we were able to meet the deadline. The one thing that I have kept with me from my days at Pixar is what Steve Jobs used to tell us: "It's all about the story. No technology can fix a bad story."

A Whole New World

After Pixar, I started my own company, where I learned a lot of my business skills without having to do an MBA. When I saw video becoming the next paradigm shift on the internet, I joined Google and moved to Youtube.

My role was technical, and it was about forging partnerships. Youtube enabled everyone to be a storyteller and publish their thoughts and stories online. But how do they get the audience they're looking for, target for revenue and make a sustainable business for themselves? That's what my team and I helped creators with - what we now call the 'creator economy'.

Around 2016, I started seeing another trend. The appetite for watching content on TVs was back, this time via streaming services. That's what made me take up a leadership role at Google for TV. I crafted the strategy and we are now executing on bringing our platforms to TV, so that everyone can lean back and enjoy YouTube, Netflix, Hotstar and more in their living rooms.

It was quite an entrepreneurial journey, within Google, convincing our execs for the need to invest in this space. The art of storytelling helped me along the way. I was mindful of my audiences and convincing them about what we need to do and why.

We launched GoogleTV a few years ago to great fanfare and continue the momentum for this product today, where it has become a full fledged business of its own.

Building Great Products

Right after I left Pixar, Raj said, "Hey, I'm going to learn computer graphics too. Can you help me?" We tried finding books but they were either too basic or too advanced. That's what inspired us to co-author the book 'Learning Computer Graphics', published by Springer. We were thrilled when it was used by many universities as an introductory course.

Looking back, I think the best reason to build something is because you want it. A certain kind of content, a certain type of experience - you build

RAPID FIRE

I believe: That everyone has a voice.

If I could, I would: Go to Africa on a safari.

I love: Being with my family. I love Bollywood and I love Bollywood weddings.

The world needs: More diversity of opinions and diversity of thinking.

I'm passionate about: Media and the power of it.

Success is: Being content and being happy with yourself.

The most important thing to remember when I step into work? To have fun.

it and find the rest of the world wants it too.

Challenges as a Woman

Being the only woman in the room is always a hard challenge. Especially if you're junior, it's sometimes really hard to speak up and to feel heard. Now that I am a senior, my role is to be an ally to the next generation workforce. To make sure the voices of younger women are heard. Because in the end, the best businesses are built when there's diversity of thought.

Work-Life Balance

There is a Pixar movie called 'Cars' where the protagonist, Lightning McQueen, wants to race from one end of the country to the other. But he ends up on Route 66, he slows down and makes a bunch of friends there. The friendships lead him to greater heights in the end. For me, that is such a compelling narrative for your career journey..

Sometimes, you're going down that highway really, really fast. So fast that you don't even have time to smell the roses. Then there are times when you slow down and take an exit. At Pixar, I was in the accelerated mode. In fact, I was expecting Sonal while working on 'A Bug's Life'. If you see the end-credits, there's a section called 'production babies'. Sonal is one of the ten in that list!

After that, I went part time for a few years, left work completely for a year and got back on, without feeling like I had lost out on anything. Of course, it's never easy. Like all women, I have felt guilty going to an important meeting when my kids wanted me to be at home. One thing that helps is that the products I work on are products that my kids love and relate to.

My daughter Sonal is working at a biotech company, Genentech, while my son Ronak is a sophomore in computer science and business at USC. Recently, Sonal told me, "Mom, I'm so inspired by the fact that you continued to work and have us kids and did a good job of raising us. That inspires me to want to also do the same." What more can I ask for?

Biking with husband, Raj Pai, staying strong and fit

Aaj phir se
aaloo??

IN HER ELEMENT

I have one leg in science and one leg in culture, bringing them together has been my calling.

Early Life

I always had this rather adventurous streak, coupled with an interest in science. The scientific influence came from my father, Dr M.R. Srinivasan, who is an eminent nuclear engineer. When we were young, he used to take us to reactor sites and explain the process of nuclear fusion and fission. But we also visited a lot of historical sites and monuments. In the early 70s, we lived right next to Mahabalipuram as my father was working on the Kalpakkam nuclear power plant. I remember running around all those Pallava monuments. My mother, Geetha, was the head of the World Wildlife Fund in India. She is a very adventurous lady. In 1987, just after IIT, I went with her on a trek cum pilgrimage to see the ice stalactite worshipped as a Shiva lingam in snow-bound Amarnath in Kashmir. I was also a student of Bharatnatyam from the age of 9 and trained under several renowned gurus. So, I was exposed to the intangible cultural and natural heritage of India.

However, it was physics and astronomy that I was most drawn to. I loved stargazing, it was so exciting in those days to visit the Nehru Planetarium. I also remember my father taking me to the Radio Astronomy centre of TIFR in Ooty which had so many telescopes.

Being a topper in school with an interest in science, I wrote the IIT JEE exam. But I was not nerdily obsessed with studying for, or getting into IIT. So it was a pleasant surprise that my JEE rank was in the 400s. By a lucky coincidence, when I joined, a new option for B.Tech. was being offered i.e. Engineering Physics. It seemed an ideal one for me.

PADMA SHRI DR. SHARADA SRINIVASAN

B.Tech, Engineering Physics, 1987

Professor, National Institute of Advanced Studies, Bangalore
Honorary Fellow, University of Exeter, UK

Prof Sharada Srinivasan after receiving Padmashri Award at Rashtrapati Bhavan, New Delhi In March 2019, seen with mother Geetha Srinivasan, husband Digvijay Mallah and daughter Lasya

Life at IIT Bombay

IIT provided a lot of scope for diverse, eclectic experiences. For example, I used to enjoy doing welding. Making a good metallograph is not just science, it's an art as well. There is a beautiful verse by 12th century Kannada poetess Akka Mahadevi who says, 'Weld so that the weld may not be seen'. Which adds a metaphysical aspect to it.

In humanities we had an elective called 'postcolonial literature' where we read Wole Soyinka and Chinua Achebe. At the annual performing arts festival I did a choreography set to Philip Glass's music of Koyaanisqatsi, which is the Hopi Indian word for 'life out of balance'. It was an apt metaphor that stayed with me. There is a need to regain balance, whether between humans and the environment, or between science and culture.

Along with four batchmates, I worked on, acted in and choreographed for the English feature film, 'Nuclear Winter'. The film expressed the concerns of students at the prospect of a nuclear holocaust in the Cold War years. Shot on the IIT campus, it was directed by Zul Vellani and screened on Doordarshan, with the cast including Vijay Crishna.

Sharada performing Bharatanatyam dance photo from event in the late 80's

> **IIT BOMBAY, TO ME IS: ABOUT COMING OF AGE AND THEN STEPPING OUT OF YOUR COMFORT ZONE.**

Being a part of the H10 sisterhood was a special experience. As women, we were encouraged to challenge ourselves and do adventurous things like mountaineering, and even rappelling down the H10 wall!

While pursuing my B.Tech. I realized that my interest lay in application, not pure science. My father, who had worked with Homi Bhabha, always talked about nuclear power as a tool for development. I was also influenced by my uncle C.V. Seshadri, an IIT Kanpur professor who used technology for rural upliftment.

While at IIT, I used to spend time in a tribal block of Karjat, doing appropriate technology documentation. At the back of my mind was the idea of making a connect with the grassroots and our traditional knowledge systems.

Professional Journey

Engineering Physics put a lot of emphasis on materials science, for example semiconductors, and exposed me to techniques of spectroscopic analysis. Eventually that's where my career went. I read a paper on the use of spectrochemical analysis in archaeology and became very interested in where that could take us.

I decided to explore the applications of scientific techniques in studying

Sharada performing Bharatanatyam dance in 2012 in Lyon, depicting the connection of the star Arudra/ Betelguese in the constellation Orion with Siva Nataraja

Sharada in Bharatanatyam dance pose depicting Siva Nataraja in the 90s

art history and archaeology. So I pursued an M.A. in Arts and Archaeology at the University of London, followed by a PhD in Archaeometallurgy at Institute of Archaeology, University College London.

My thesis was titled: 'The enigma of the dancing 'pancha-loha' (five-metalled) icons'. I used lead isotope analysis, compositional and trace element analysis and ore-artefact analysis for finger-printing medieval South Indian statuary bronzes sampled from Victoria and Albert Museum London, Government Museum, Chennai and the British Museum.

As a Bharatanatyam dancer, I was always fascinated with Nataraja. We even perform a dance where we describe the Panchbhuta - the five elements which constitute the Dancing Shiva. So I was intrigued about the actual elemental analysis and what it could tell us about the history of technology of alloys and metals used in antiquity.

Looking at the materials characterization also helps in terms of the archaeological understanding. For instance, it is difficult to authenticate Chola bronzes because there were so many of them, produced by similar techniques over hundreds of years. Chemical profiling helps to create a kind of fingerprint by which you can tell apart bronzes of later periods from earlier periods.

Pushing Boundaries

The technique that I use in particular is known as lead Isotope ratio analysis because of the fact that the lead sources have distinct isotopic proportions which can be traced back to the source.

Often, I get described as an archaeo-metallurgist, as what we do is look at evidence of ancient mining and metallurgy.

Since NIAS is adjacent to the Indian Institute of Science, we have access to labs. We use a variety of techniques from X-ray analysis to electron microscopy to understand the metal microstructure. It's exciting to unravel how a blacksmith worked centuries ago, leaving a distinct fingerprint. For me, the moment of discovery is an Indiana Jones kind of moment.

Because I'm working in an area which is not fashionable or mainstream, it is always a challenge to get funding. So being recognised by one's peers has definitely been very fulfilling. I have one leg in science and one leg in culture - bringing to-

Prof. Sharada Srinivasan at father Dr. M.R Srinivasan's 90th birthday party on 5th Jan 2020 in Bangalore, seen with him, mother Geetha, daughter Lasya, brother Raghuvir Srinivasan and his wife Satu Pekki

gether these two diverse fields has been my calling. That keeps me on my feet, keeps the motivation going.

RAPID FIRE

I believe: You don't have to follow the script.
If I could, I would: Love to go back and cycle around the IIT Bombay campus.
I'm passionate about: Bridging the science and the culture divide.
I wish: I could set up a metal museum.
If you fall: Pick yourself up with grace.
Success is: Sweeter if you take the road less travelled.

Work-Life Balance

I am high-strung, whereas my husband Digvijay is calm and collected. He owns and manages his family-owned tea estates in Coonoor and Ooty and is a keen photographer. He has always been very broad-minded and supportive of my professional demands, especially when I've had to undertake international travel and archaeological fieldwork. He was happy to look after our daughter Lasya when I was away, so in that sense he's been a new age husband.

Like any working mother, I have felt guilty about not spending enough time with my daughter. When she was just two, I had a major field trip to the

fascinating Harappan site of Dholavira in the Rann of Kutch. During her vacations, we would undertake holiday-cum-fieldwork visits as a family. For instance, we spent time in Aranmula documenting the metal mirror-making workshops and taking the kettuvalam boats across the backwaters in Kerala.

In 2019, we were in the hospital as my daughter was very ill when I got a call. "Madam… hello… I'd like to tell you that you've been awarded the Padma Shri. Would you like to accept?" Luckily, my daughter recovered fully and the full import of the award struck me when my phone began to ring non-stop.

Challenges as a Woman

Being in a male-dominated environment like IIT, you learn to kind of stand up for yourself. That really stands you in good stead, no matter what you do in life.

STEM is male-dominated. Additionally, archaeology involves travel to remote places.

I remember once I had to visit a mining site in Guntur for fieldwork. I wrote to the officer, he said, please come. When I landed up there, he bit taken aback - he wasn't expecting Dr Sharada Srinivasan to be a woman. He then made arrangements for a separate room for me and so on. On that visit, I also recall a cheetah which literally leaped out of an old, working mine! Sadly, it happened so fast I could not press my finger on the camera button.

Advice to Young Women

You don't have to have the perfect answers or know everything you want to do. When I was 18, if somebody had told me I would have had an inclination towards archeology, I would have laughed. Life does teach you and you learn as you go along. So it's okay to be open ended about things, even indecisive.

AWARDS & HONOURS

- Elected to the American Academy of Arts and Sciences - 2021.
- Padma Shri - 2019.
- Dr Kalpana Chawla Young Women's Scientist Award - 2011.
- Materials Research Society of India (MRSI) Medal - 2006.

POWER OF DREAMS

My left brain and right brain work in tandem to build innovative software products.

Early Life

One of my favorite things, when I was little, was to watch a cartoon show called 'The Jetsons'. It was about this future age where you had flying cars and robots doing all the work. I dreamt that at some point, this would become a reality. The way technology can transform our world has always fascinated me and I am interested in work of this type even today.

I grew up in a very scientific environment. Education was a high priority in my family. My father was a famous scientist while my mom was very artistic, very creative. I loved my math and science, I also loved my art and doing different types of creative things.

When I had to choose after 12th standard, I was debating whether to take up medicine or engineering. My older brother Anurag and sister Shalini had both joined IIT Bombay and were great role models. Seeing how happy they were at IIT, I too decided to choose this path.

Life at IIT Bombay

The IIT years were an amazing four years of my life. I really enjoyed the classes. I was not the kind who would stay up late and study all night. I valued having a very balanced time in terms of studying, building close friendships, philosophizing about the future of the world as we knew it then and taking part in different activities on campus. I was part of the institute's table tennis team, as well as several other activities.

We were a small group of women. As a result, we formed closer, deeper relationships. It was hard for some of the women, as in some branches there was just one girl in the class. So, if she wanted to study, there was no support system in the hostel. For-

SHIVANI GOVIL

B.Tech, Chem Engg, 1992

Chief Product Officer, CCC Intelligent Solutions

"Do not feel intimidated by anyone."
Family Times

Friends forever

tunately, for me, in chemical engineering, we had six other women so we had a good support group.

Being a small group of women had its pros and cons. We often got targeted for pranks. One in particular, I remember, was when I was working really hard on my B.Tech. project and somebody played a prank on me and deleted all my data. It was the end of the semester so I was quite panicked. But I was able to get the data restored, and it taught me that no problem in life is so difficult that it can't be solved.

"

IIT BOMBAY, TO ME IS: A FAMILY AND A HOME.

I met my husband Joe at IITB. We were both in the same department and got to know each other well.

Professional Journey

After graduating, I went to Princeton University for my Master's in Chemical Engineering. I found myself fascinated by both engineering and public policy topics. Although the subject was not offered by my department, when I spoke to the Dean, he was supportive. He created a research project so that I could work on environmental policies impacting electric utilities - a topic that I think is so relevant to what we see in the world today.

That was the start of the journey where I realized that you don't always have to follow a certain path. If you start dreaming, people will come together to support you, to make

your dreams happen. While working in environmental policy I got fascinated by strategy and how businesses think and operate. And that led me to my career in management consulting with Andersen.

After a few years of being in the US, I felt very strongly about giving back to India. I wanted to quit my job in the US to go and work with the Environmental Ministry in India, to help reduce emissions.

When I shared that with a partner in my firm, Barbara, she said, "I'm going to support you". She created that opportunity for me. And working through a big company, I was able to drive a bigger impact than what I would have been able to do by myself. This again underlined for me that if you dream big, things can happen.

We moved to Silicon Valley in the late 90s and being in the Valley, I wanted to experience working in a startup. I worked in two Silicon Valley startups and that's where I truly started to appreciate the power of combining technology and customer insight, to build great products.

I moved to SAP in 2007, where my focus was on how to apply technology and innovation to solve people's pain points – to build the future that you want to see. That is what I continue to do, even today.

Design Thinking

As Chief Product Officer at CCC Intelligent Solutions, I'm responsible for our entire product strategy and portfolio – we build AI driven products for the automotive industry. I also wear a dual hat of being the Chief Marketing Officer at the company. This allows me to use my left brain and my right brain - my technology skills, as well as my creativity - as we build and design these products.

Getting into an automotive accident is very stressful. The key question we solve is - how can we use technology to resolve the adverse incident? The goal is to help you move on with your life, as seamlessly as possible. Whether it is repairing your car, buying a new car or anything else, you don't have to figure it out. The technology will do it for you.

I am proud of our entire product portfolio. One of the innovative new products that we launched in 2022 was called 'Estimate STP'. If you get into an accident, all you need to do is take a picture. Using AI, we can immediately tell you what's the extent

Life, Travel and Journeys

of the damage, how much it will cost to fix it (based on the year, make, model, etc) and where you can take the vehicle for repair. This product was featured as one of the ten coolest innovations of 2021, alongside products from NASA and MIT.

My experience in consulting really helped me look at a new industry and quickly come to an understanding of what's important and then how do you solve for that.

RAPID FIRE

I believe in: The power of dreams.
If I could, I would: Travel around the world.
The world needs more: Empathy.
I'm passionate about: Applying technology to create a better future for all of us.
If you fall?: I land among the stars.
Success is: Being at peace.
One thing I wish, somebody had told me when I was 18: Dream big, make mistakes, learn and move on.

Challenges as a Woman

In the early part of my career, I would often be the only woman in a meeting. But coming from the almost-all male IIT campus, I never felt uncomfortable or awkward speaking up. I remember being in a meeting with a leading tech company in the Bay Area and found that even though I was the seniormost person from my company, the other company personnel were just talking to the men in my team. I had to assert myself and 'lean in' to be part of the discussion.

A big challenge we all face is balancing across all the different parts of life – our families (children, parents, extended family), our career, and also making time for ourselves. What I have found is that it's not an either/ or. You have to develop a system that allows you to flow with what is most important at that phase of your life. Also, you need a support

network, to help you along the way.
I believe that in everything you do, people are at the heart of it. How you treat others and how you make them feel is so important - relationships define how much people are willing to support each other.

Work-Life Balance

My husband has been my strong partner, throughout my journey. We have both taken turns to make family life work. At different times, one of us would have to put more emphasis on work and the other would pick up the slack on other fronts. He's been my rock and anchor throughout. He's also a very jovial person. He brings joy and fun to the family and makes me laugh a lot, which is hugely important, given all the stress that we go through in life.
My daughters, Megan and Ria, inspire me to do so much and think differently. When I was working in the mobile field, Megan was a teenager. She would show me apps she came across and tell me how I could apply them to my work. My younger daughter, Ria, is also extremely talented, both academically and creatively.
I remember, once we were painting together and I wasn't happy with my brushstrokes and asked her to do it for me. She said, "It's no big deal. If you spoil it, you can just do it again. It's okay to make mistakes. You can always fix them and move on." That day, she taught me a very important lesson!
Also, our dog Goldie provides constant love that keeps us laughing and smiling – no matter how bad the weather may be.

Sisters

Advice to Young Women

I am so excited for what the future holds for young women today. There are so many more opportunities! I encourage women to dream big and embrace the life they want to choose. People think of STEM as very binary – that you have to be analytical, you have to be very technical and you have to do hard, quantitative things. But I think that to truly succeed you need to be multidimensional.
My advice to young women is, do not feel intimidated by anyone. Bring your whole self and set of passions, and take time to explore how you can fit all of that together to do what gives you joy. You will find that the world is vast and that each person has a unique set of skills that add value in a different way.
Diverse teams are the most successful and you as an individual bring a lot of value to any team, with your unique combination of skills and interests.

OPEN SESAME

My first exposure to biomedical applications started at IITB, as my B.Tech. project was focused on drug delivery.

Early Life

I was in Mumbai when I was very young but my parents moved to Chennai when I was in 2nd standard. I always enjoyed math and chemistry but I didn't really have any engineers in my family. So I didn't have a whole lot of background in terms of encouraging me to go into engineering. But education was always given a lot of importance in my family. I studied in Adarsh Vidyalaya until 10th standard and in P.S. Senior Secondary School for class 11 and 12. My parents have been a wonderful influence on my life, and my

DR. SURYA MALLAPRAGADA

B.Tech, Chemical Engineering, 1993

Associate Vice President for Research at Iowa State University

Anson Marston Distinguished Professor, and Carol Vohs Chair Professor of Chemical and Biological Engineering

Surya Mallapragada holding a vial of nanoparticles
(image credit: Dan McClanahan)

"In research... there are lots of unknowns."

Surya Mallapragada with husband Balaji Narasimhan, also an IITB alum

father especially always told me, "Just let us know what you want to do, we'll support you in that". My parents were my inspiration.

When the JEE result came, I ranked in the mid-600s. It would have been natural for me to join IIT Madras but IIT Bombay was the best for chemical engineering, so I chose Bombay.

Life at IIT Bombay

I was 16 when I left home and it was definitely a very life-changing experience. I credit my current success to my IITB days and everything that I have learned, not just from my professors, but from friends and peers. And it's not just chemical engineering but how to live your life.

We had 17 girls in our batch, which was one of the highest at that time. We were extremely close and we still are. We even had a name for our group of 17 – 'Nizzies'. In my chemical engineering class, there were four women, which was much more than in other disciplines. We supported each other quite a bit.

In my first year, I stayed back during the Diwali break while most of the students had gone home. So we hung out near the Vihar Lake and suddenly, a dog bit me and ran away. I had to get 14 rabies shots in my tummy which was not at all pleasant. I'm working on vaccines now, in part due to this personal experience of having

> "
>
> **IIT BOMBAY, TO ME IS: AN EXTREMELY IMPORTANT, FORMATIVE EXPERIENCE IN MY LIFE.**

to take a sub-optimal and painful rabies vaccine.

I completed my seminar project in my 3rd year with Dr. Bellare. My B.Tech. project in the 4th year with Dr Suresh was actually related to drug delivery. I really enjoyed both experiences with my two mentors and wanted to continue doing research in this area.

That's why I decided to go to Purdue where I had a wonderful mentor for my PhD, Dr Nicholas Peppas. My postdoctoral advisor at MIT was Prof. Bob Langer, who went on to co-found Moderna. Both my mentors had this wonderful mindset that you have to work on problems that are important and make an impact.

Professional Journey

My work mostly focuses on materials for biomedical applications. My first significant exposure to working on biomedical applications started at IITB, as my B.Tech. project was focused on drug delivery. My interest area is biomaterial development for different biomedical applications, such as drug delivery, neural tissue engineering and vaccines.

Conventional vaccines are made from live or inactivated viruses whereas mRNA vaccines use mRNA and lipids. Similarly, in our work, we take proteins from the pathogen and put them in polymer nanoparticles. So it's essentially a virus- mimicking particle, if you will. What we are trying to do is to change the degradation rate so that there is slow release of this protein to get longer immunity.

Like mRNA vaccines, it's more of a platform technology which can be used to target a variety of pathogens. Right now, we're working on what we hope is a universal influenza nanovaccine to provide long lasting protection. Our vaccine work is a collaborative effort with my husband Balaji Narasimhan, who is also an IITB graduate.

Another area close to my heart is neural tissue engineering. Can we electrically stimulate stem cells to get them into one state or another, such that they are able to regenerate? We track various cellular parameters with sensors in real time to understand this. And then the idea is to use the data to build models and make sense of it all.

I'm an introvert, according to the Myers-Briggs test. But you evolve with time, right? Going in front of a class and teaching, and also handling administration duties, has forced me to get out of my comfort zone to some extent.

Innovator Mindset

All my projects are collaborative and interdisciplinary, this has been a very rewarding experience. To give you an example, just last year, we moved into a new research space at Iowa State University, which is on the fifth floor of a building. It's an open lab concept where we have chemical engineers, immunologists, neuroscientists - people from many different backgrounds.

We've seen the magic of the graduate students working all together, talking to each other over coffee or something like that, to see if new avenues of research result. So promot-

Surya Mallapragada presenting a talk on her research

RAPID FIRE

I believe: That hard work pays off.
If I could, I would: Love to spend more time with my kids.
The world needs: More women engineers.
I'm passionate about: My research.
The stuff I don't sweat: Things that are outside your control.
Success is: A team sport.

ing an environment which allows for that exchange of ideas is important. The key is a problem solving mindset. It really doesn't matter what aspect you come to this problem from, there are so many different ways you can try to solve it. For instance, some of our patents focus on development of new polymeric biomaterials that are specifically designed to be ideal drug delivery carriers and overcome the limitations of existing technologies.

With research, it's delayed gratification because things take time to come to fruition. And then you have the teaching part. That's instant gratification. So I think I have the best of both worlds to keep me going. Also, anything new that you develop, you have to look at it from an ethical, legal and social standpoint.

Work-Life Balance

My husband is also from IIT Bombay, chemical engineering, one year my senior. But I didn't know him well when I was on campus. Only when I was accepted to grad school at Purdue, I reached out to him. He had just started graduate school at Purdue the previous year. He was my only contact and he came to pick me up at the airport. 11 years later, we were married!

When we decided to have kids, I had already been promoted to full professor. My kids are in high school right now, so they're still at home. It's always a juggling effort with their after-school activities and looking at my own calendar and things like that. But I just decided to use the time-honored method where grandparents help out. So my parents have been living with me for the last few years. Prior to having kids, I had more time for hobbies. Right now, the kids are involved in several activities, so that takes up a lot of time and provides us a great deal of enjoyment.

Advice to Young Women

Believe in yourself. There were times when I doubted myself but I had a great support system in my parents and friends and that pushed me in the right direction.

With a chemical engineering degree, you can do so many different things, you can go into the semiconductor industry, go into the traditional petrochemicals or alternative fuels like biofuels, vaccines or human health – the opportunities are unlimited. We're working on how to deliver combination therapies for pancreatic cancer, for instance.

There are so many different important problems that you can work on. But remember that in research, you don't know if things will work or not. There are lots of unknowns.

AWARDS & HONOURS

- Elected Top 100 young innovators in MIT Technology Review magazine.
- National Science Foundation CAREER award.
- Young Alumni Achievement award, IITB.
- Fellow, National Academy of Inventors.
- Foreign Fellow, National Academy of Sciences India.
- Fellow of the American Institute of Chemical Engineers, the American Association for the Advancement of Science, the International Academy of Medical and Biological Engineering, the American Institute of Medical and Biological Engineering.

FINANCE FEMME

I realised that economics only has problems, with no universal formulas or easy solutions.

Early Life

I grew up in an extremely cloistered, protected environment because my family was based out of Kuwait, which is one of the more conservative of the Middle Eastern countries. As a young person growing up, I didn't have the kind of freedom that similar people of my age would have had in a country like India.

My father worked at the Public Works Department as a draughtsman on the design of buildings. My mother was a biology teacher. I have three younger sisters. At the Indian School in Kuwait I was a good student, in terms of getting marks. But I was argumentative and wanted answers to everything, even those things that were to be taken for granted.

I had a book on 100 greatest personalities which had everyone from Jesus Christ to Madam Curie. Sandwiched between Christ (#1) and Prophet Mohammed (#3) was Issac Newton. I was fascinated by Newton because it seemed that his way to fame and glory was through the path of research, establishing facts that could not be disputed.

I decided I must do research too.

But people told me that there is no career in research, you need to be practical and get a job. And the only career choices for good students of those days were medicine or engineering. Which is where civil engineering at IIT came in. As one of my relatives put it, "There will always be the need to build roads, bridges and homes."

Life at IIT Bombay

IIT taught me about winning and losing. Before coming to IIT, I was an academic star. Here, I was barely able to hold my head above the water. And I wondered, is there some-

DR. SUSAN THOMAS

B.Tech, Civil Engineering, 1989

Research Professor of Business, Jindal Global University
Senior Research Fellow and Co-Founder at XKDR Forum, Bombay

"Constantly challenge yourself."

Family ties, present and next gen

thing wrong with me? I remember an uncle of mine asked me, "Are you on drugs?" But no, IIT grading was just hard. So there were times when I failed and I learnt it's not the end of the world.

IIT gave me a sense of freedom. I learnt to ride a bike, travel late night in local trains. It taught me how to be a much more well-rounded individual, thinking big thoughts. There were many conversations which I think were guides on how to live life and how to do research that played out over the long horizon of my life, not just the years that I was at the institute.

> "
>
> **IIT BOMBAY, TO ME IS: FUN AND FREEDOM AND A LOT OF LEARNING.**

The freedom to explore everything was all-pervasive. I remember that we once loaded a program in the computer lab which mimicked the login and password screen but which locked the machine. There was mayhem for a while, with users going crazy, wondering how to get in. After it was discovered, the person running the lab shrugged it off as a harmless prank.

IIT was a space to grow up, being guided by sage and seasoned mentors. Professors like Dr. Pathak of the Computer Science department and Prof. Shevare at the Aeronautical department treated us not like children but as young adults. We learned how it was always important to apply the mind in all situations, and that developing judgement was a critical part of growing up.

I once worked as a Teaching Assistant (TA) for Prof.Pathak. He hauled me up because I gave all groups either a 10 or a 0 in their assignments, pointing out that may be the easy path for me but that grades had to reflect the more nuanced aspects of the work that was done. It was a lesson I will never forget.

The Big Switch

In civil engineering, we learned how to build roads, buildings and bridges. But then, in the library there were reams and reams of volumes to help you figure out the right thickness of steel girders and the width of the right thickness concrete columns for the actual structures, where all our careful calculations were scaled up by a safety factor of 3!

I thought, naively, that civil engineering has a solution for everything with little innovation to be found. So if I wanted to go into a life of research, I needed to look for a new domain. We had elective classes at IIT where Prof. Bidkar introduced me to economics research. And I realised that economics only had problems, with no universal formulas or library lookup solutions.

I concluded that I need to be an economist and joined the PhD program at the University of Southern California in Los Angeles. But as a B.Tech., I had to make up by taking all the

When phones were wired and numbers were stored on paper

undergraduate economics courses I had missed. In a couple of years, I had done enough courses to get a master's in economics and start the PhD program.

I met my future husband Ajay at IIT; his sister, Sadhana, was my batchmate. Ajay's father was an economist, and he himself is a walking, talking Wikipedia on the subject. It was yet another reason to spend time together, talk, argue and bond. When he graduated from IIT, he was admitted to the economics program at USC. A couple of years later, I joined him there as well.

Professional Journey

I have always been an academic. After getting my PhD in economics, I presented my paper at the Indira Gandhi Institute of Development Research in Bombay. And the director, Dr. Kirit Parikh, offered me a job after that. Teaching and doing research at the IGIDR was what I did for the longest time.

My research work is in finance and markets – the microstructure of financial markets including institutions, laws and who are the users of markets, household finance, finance and firms, government contracting and understanding how courts work. It started off as technical, academic research, and has today become a mix of policy and quantitative research.

As an academic in Bombay, I could explore both the edges of what was known in my field, as well as get it tested against other academics, experts working in financial firms and policy makers who were constantly thinking about new developments and reforms in India.

The most recent policy engagement was being a member of the Bankruptcy Legislative Reform Committee set up by the Ministry of Finance in 2014, chaired by Dr. T. K. Viswanathan, who was previously Secretary in the Ministry of Law and Justice. I led a group of economic and legal scholars in drafting a bill that the committee submitted to the Ministry of Finance in 2015.

The committee's draft was enacted as the Insolvency and Bankruptcy Code in 2016. This was a sea-change in how insolvency – the failure to repay a loan – was resolved all over the country. This code is a single law across India for both individuals as well as companies, setting the legal process to be followed when a loan repayment has failed.

I was also a member of the Working Committee of the Ministry of Corpo-

RAPID FIRE

I believe: That when things get really bad, we (the human race) will fix it.
If I could, I would: Gift everyone a sense of humor.
I love: Designing a problem.
The world needs: More trees and forests.
I wish: People would think before they speak
The stuff I don't sweat: Clothes
Success is: Something that allows me to do more of what I do.
One thing I wish somebody had told me when I was 18: To write more.

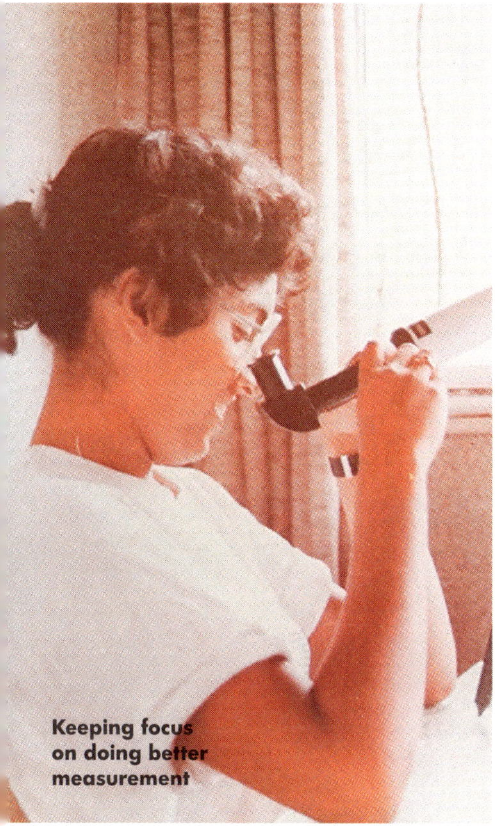

Keeping focus on doing better measurement

rate Affairs to build the Insolvency and Bankruptcy Board, the regulator for this code.

Challenges as a Woman

I have spent a large part of my working life in the field of financial markets. Like all other areas, there is a strong gender bias, which was stronger in the late 1990s, relative to the more recent period of 2022 when there have been several policy efforts to correct for the bias through legal and regulatory interventions.

But finance is also a technical area with a mix of maths, stats, computational and finance knowledge. When there are such objective requirements, it can be easier to overcome gender biases because the knowledge can be more visible than in other softer sciences. I had developed a lot of the technical computational and statistical skills of finance during my PhD.

These helped establish my role when I was interacting with the industry and policy makers in the financial sector in India. In the mid-90s, financial markets were a small part of the economic landscape in India and tangible skills were highly valued, particularly in the academic and research domain.

Advice to Young Women

Firstly, learn your subjects well. Constantly challenge yourself that if you were given the chance, what is the solution that you would propose and don't stop yourself from asking that question just because you are young, you don't have that job. STEM gives you the tools and the discipline you need to chase down a fact and make it defensible before you put it into a policy.

But remember, we are living in a society. So try to understand the people. Read literature, history and philosophy because that's going to define the context in which you will apply tools.

CHANGING LIVES

To work in the field of development, you need to cultivate the fine art of empathy.

Early Life

I grew up on the Osmania University campus in Hyderabad. My father was a professor of French language, while my mom was a professor of Psychology. We lived on the campus, with huge open spaces and lots of trees. Life was simple and we had a routine of walking to school (co-education till 7th standard), back home, then homework, followed by playing outdoors.

We spoke Marathi at home and grew up with a grandmother, a grandaunt, uncles and aunts. We are three siblings - Harsha, Srinivas and me (Srinivas and I are twins). Growing up with brothers, I preferred games that boys play such as marbles and gilli danda, more than the games that girls play such as hopscotch and skipping.

When Srinivas and I passed our 12th standard exams with high marks and secured a national state merit scholarship, I remember my father telling us, "The nation is investing a lot in you and your education and this comes with a responsibility. It would be good if the country gets a very high return on the investment it is making on my children".

I must confess I did not quite understand this as a teenager! But somewhere that advice stuck with me. And my journey has shaped up in a way that has lived up to those words.

Life at IIT Bombay

Majorly, the influences have all been my hostel mates, who were all doing such daring things. And I thought, well, if they can do it, I can try to do it too. We fought to have the same rules for girls and boys (such as hostel timings for girls, allowing male

SVATI BHOGLE

M.Tech, Chemical Engineering, 1981

CEO, Technology Informatics Design Endeavor (TIDE)

Founder, Sustaintech India

President, Clean Energy Access Network

"Cultivate the fine art of empathy."

Responding to questions at an annual India Energy Access Summit

Svati with grandchildren Mihir, Tarrini, Roshni, Dia and Aditya

friends inside our hostel) and made it happen.

The late night cack sessions at IIT taught me that you must listen to other points of view, that you're not always right. You have to respect diversity of opinion and diversity of cultures and also build relationships with people who are from different social classes and backgrounds.

I was the mess secretary in the hostel, which was quite challenging. One day, at about five in the morning, the mess workers came to me and said, "We are going on strike today". Thinking on my feet I said, "Okay, no problem, I'll make chai for you". And I actually did that.

After sending them off, I remember there were 4-5 girls who'd woken up early to study. And I said, "Chalo, let's make breakfast!" (boiled eggs and bread) and lunch (rice and dal). The next day at 5 a.m. the mess workers woke me up and said, "We are on strike again today but food has been cooked".

We found many creative ways of having really low-cost fun. We used to go to the chemistry lab at midnight and bake cakes with 170 grams maida, 170 grams of sugar, some butter and eggs. The next morning the ovens for drying glassware would be smelling of cinnamon!

"

IIT BOMBAY, TO ME IS: THAT FEELING THAT I'VE COME BACK HOME.

Professional Journey

I am a development practitioner. This means that I identify problems faced by rural communities, largely around energy, environment and livelihoods through a participatory process. And then, we develop technology solutions that meet their needs.

My first project was on the domestic cookstove or chulha for household cooking. I worked at the centre for Application of Science and Technology for Rural Areas conceived by Prof. Amulya Reddy at the Indian Institute of Science. Prof. Lokras and Prof. Kumar in the department of Chemical Engineering guided us in the design of the wood burning stoves.

After that, for about a decade, I took a partial break because I had two small children. In the meantime, some of my former colleagues had started TIDE. My dilemma then was, should I move from a prestigious institution to a fledgling non-profit? I took the plunge and was elevated to CEO within a few months of joining. That's when my professional journey actually began.

Over two years, we developed and demonstrated energy-efficient solutions for ten rural industry clusters. This included jaggery-making, herbal medicine preparation, textile bleaching, dyeing, rubber vulcanisation, pottery firing, etc. All of them used firewood as fuel and we redesigned the stoves, to reduce firewood consumption and emissions.

We modified energy consumption patterns in the informal rural business sector, saving 30-40% fuel. Our model was to transfer technology to grassroots enterprises, training them and helping them with marketing and raising small funds.

Later, we launched a project for energy efficiency in the tea industry. In three years about 65% of tea factories accepted our recommendations. 100,000 tons of CO_2 was saved per year, through these interventions.

Opening plenary of the India Clean Cooking Forum, Delhi 2016

Demonstrating an innovative heat energy product to the Secretary DST and other scientists in Forest Research Institute, Dehradun

Challenge Accepted

I remember a long conversation with Prof. Mukunda of Indian Institute of Science at Chennai Airport in 2008. He urged me to start a social enterprise with a for-profit objective, as most ideas which scaled up had a profit motive. He said, "You've played your first innings, now go into the second."

Around the same time, I noticed a Michael Jordan poster in my son's room which said, "I can accept failure but I cannot accept not trying". I think these two messages helped resolve my dilemma. We started a for-profit company, Sustaintech, to scale the work of our NGO.

Our goal is rapid replication in the commercial cookstove sector. If a dhaba buys our chulha for Rs 10-15k or even 50k, the fuel saving alone pays back the investment. Since I understood heat transfer, we were able to design stoves for specific uses like roasting, frying, tea-making, etc.

We engage with grassroots communities, not only because their wisdom is very important to us, but

RAPID FIRE

I believe: Living in the present not the past or future.

If I could, I would: Dream big and be more ambitious.

I'm passionate about: Spending time in forests and nature.

The stuff I don't sweat? I don't really care what people think about me.

Success is: If you're able to wipe a tear or bring a smile to somebody's face.

One thing I wish, somebody had told me when I was 18: You're not in a rat race. Just compete with yourself.

because it reduces the time it takes for our products to go-to-market. The process is called participatory technology development. It requires engaging with potential users of our products, meeting women, youth and others to understand their needs and usage patterns. One of our illiterate grassroots women entrepreneurs - Lalita Bai - used to go from village to village, constructing stoves in people's houses. She was selected for the 'Women Transforming India Award' by Niti Aayog. That was truly very satisfying for me.

Work-Life Balance

To be productive in the peak reproductive period is a challenge for most women. I still think I took the right decision by spending those ten years working part time. Luckily, I was associated with the Karnataka State Council for Science and Technology in the IISc campus, which allowed me to work any four hours in a day. Due to this, I came back with a bang and bounced back as if there had not been a career break.

I continued to lead Sustaintech until we had addressed about 2000 street food vendors' needs. I was leading TIDE for about 20 years too. When it was time to pass on the baton, I transferred responsibility to the CEOs whom I was grooming in both the organizations.

Now I am a mentor who helps out in times of crisis.

Earlier it was very hectic, raising funds for the NGO TIDE, investments for Sustaintech, business planning, meeting targets and keeping timelines. There was not enough time for reflection. Now I work 8-10 hours a day but I find time to read and to introspect. I share my insights with the organizations I have nurtured and with other development practitioners. The women at the grassroots lead difficult lives but have great hopes for the future. Whenever I go to a village and meet these women, I come back inspired.

Advice to Young Women

To work in the field of development, I think you need to cultivate the fine art of empathy. It's a hard life. A lot of travel is required. If you are the major bread winner in your family, it is certainly possible but not easy, especially in the startup phase. But it's very rewarding and you grow as a human being.

I would strongly advise you to take your own time to make a decision. Take a sabbatical or do weekends in rural areas. Understand the challenges. Because once you get into development, going back into the corporate sector may be difficult.

AWARDS & HONOURS:

- Ashden Award for Sustainable Energy - 2008.
- PARISAR PRASHASTI, state environment award given by the Government of Karnataka - 2011.
- National Award for Women's Development through Science and Technology Award - 2013.

WATER WOMAN

I take science to society, I think of it as 'human engineering'.

Early Life

I grew up in Bandra, when it was still a sleepy suburb of Bombay in the 80s. My dad was a physicist with the Bhabha Atomic Research Centre and my mom was a math and physics teacher at St. Teresa's High School in Bandra. In fact, she was a gold medallist in Chemistry. So there was no question of 'you are a girl, you can't do science'.

Both of them encouraged me academically but my father also pushed my boundaries in many other ways. Dad was a hiker, he introduced me to the beauty of the natural world. On Sundays, everyone would be watching the movie on Doordarshan. But dad would take me from Bandra to Juhu Beach on the back seat of his bicycle. He would swim in the ocean while I played on the sand. I think what I learned from my dad was a sense of wonder. And to not be afraid to explore.

My mom was more practical and pushed me to achieve in the competitive exam sense. She was the person who was convinced I could get into IIT and even predicted my exact JEE rank to the nearest 50!

Life at IIT Bombay

My mom died at the end of my first semester at IIT. So my first two years on campus were very challenging and tinged with sadness. I remember, I used to get out of bed at 8 am, just in time to run to my classes. Luckily the Physics department was the closest to H10. I went to classes in a bit of a fog and hence fell behind on the fundamentals.

I participated, somewhat reluctantly, in the inter-hostel competitions etc. Always more behind the scenes than on stage - music, costumes, that kind of thing. But even that gives confidence. It helped me as I moved to a

VEENA SRINIVASAN

B.Tech, Engineering Physics, 1995

Director, Centre for Social and Environmental Innovation

Senior Fellow at the Ashoka Trust for Research in Ecology and the Environment (ATREE)

Veena with husband Mahesh (Mech 93) and son Aman

more outward, public speaking career later on in life.

I think the fondest memories I have are of walks around campus, the late nights at Chinko's, chatting and eating Chinese food. Many, many, small moments of fun, of learning, of just hanging around. I wish I'd watched more birds on campus; now I have an interest in nature but fewer opportunities, living in a city centre.

I had joined the Engineering Physics program but quickly realised my future was not in physics. I wanted to do something more socially relevant. IIT does allow students a few electives and all of mine ended up being in the environmental space. I did my 3rd year project on air pollution modelling and 4th year project on rural electrification using solar energy.

Noticing my inclination, my thesis advisors (Prof. Anant Mahajan and Prof. Narendra Shah) took me on a

Chilling out at IITB (From top left - Depanvita, Chatterjee Rahul Magoon, Veena Srinivasan, Anamika Talwar. Sitting down - Manoj Apte and Nikhil Pednekar)

trip to rural Maharashtra. We visited a watershed which had practiced the experiment of stopping rainwater and allowing it to recharge, thereby transforming the villages and farming incomes. The place I visited was Ralegan Siddhi - which is now famous - but not much known back then.

IIT BOMBAY,TO ME IS: A PLACE WHICH MADE ME FEEL LIKE ANYTHING IS POSSIBLE.

Professional Journey

All this confirmed that I definitely wanted to do the 'science to society' interface. So when I graduated, I worked for a year with a couple of IITB faculty on various environmental topics, such as looking at the intensity of hurricanes and modelling the gas grid for Southern India. Then I went to Boston University for a Master's in Energy and Environmental Analysis. The transition from physics to a new area was quite smooth.

Subsequently, I worked with PWC and then with Enron, which was bringing natural gas to India. I wanted to make a difference but found myself inside an aggressive corporation, full of wheeler-dealers who were speculators in the energy market. It was not the place for me. I took a 95% paycut and joined the Center for Interdisciplinary Studies in Environment and Development.

Feeling the need for more domain knowledge, I joined the Emmet Interdisciplinary Program in Environment and Resources for my PhD. My thesis was around the dynamics of water supply in the city of Chennai, a case study of water resources management in a developing country urban center. Most PhD theses involve lab work, simulations and analysis of datasets. I did actual field work, which was highly unusual.

During my postdoc I developed a framework for Stanford's Global Freshwater Initiative, analyzing the nature and causes of freshwater globally. If things had gone 'as planned', I would have been in a university department somewhere in Europe or the U.S. But in 2013, we moved back to India from the US, due to a series of elder care issues in the family. Though a difficult choice careerwise, it also opened up an opportunity to think very differently.

Making an Impact

After returning to India, I joined the Ashoka Trust for Research in Ecology and the Environment (ATREE) as a Senior Fellow. By 2018, I had written a lot of cutting edge papers but it wasn't changing anything. Hence, I founded the Centre for Social and Environmental Innovation, to translate the understanding of the problem into real world solutions.

My work over the last two decades made me realize that science has the answers. But we need to factor in human behaviour and bring people together to achieve impact on the ground. In Bangalore, every major apartment complex is required to treat its own wastewater. You have 4000 decentralized wastewater treat-

Family photo at dad's Doctorate of Science Convocation in 1984 with parents and siblings Aruna Natraj and Sumathi Pundit

Field work in Arkavathy basin (2015)

ment systems but they aren't managed well, because there is no incentive for the RWA.

So one of the ideas is, what if we were able to create wastewater markets in cities? We're working with the city of Bangalore to see if the wastewater can be used commercially, so these small-scale scale wastewater treatment plants can become viable. But it requires getting many, many, different actors aligned in the same direction.

A lot of the role that I'm playing then is not to push the frontiers of science but to be the backbone, to inject the knowledge and share data to bring these actors together. Similarly, with groundwater depletion, or any other area of water management. I had to learn many new skills, from mediation to communication to design thinking.

RAPID FIRE

I believe: That as a collective, we can solve hard challenges.
If I could, I would. I would have more science in solving societal problems.
I love: Working with young pneople. They give me energy.
The world needs: More women leaders To make the world a better place.
I wish: I could give a hug to every young woman who is having a hard time in the workplace at the moment.

Challenges as a Woman

I think the first and the most important skill is a growth mindset. When I took on the director position here, I needed to manage larger teams than I was accustomed to. So I worked with an executive coach. And the phrase the coach gave me was 'holding power with grace'. I really loved that phrase because I was often in rooms where I felt intimidated.

When you go to government programs or meet senior academics - all men - they can be very blunt and insulting to your face. I've noticed that

even in conferences, only women will be asked really tough and harsh questions. 'Holding power with grace' means holding your competence, your power. But being graceful and answering with a smile even in those circumstances.

Work-Life Balance

I met my husband at IIT Bombay and got married right after my master's. My son was born during my 2nd year of PhD but that actually worked out well for me. I had a lot more time and flexibility, I even took him along for my fieldwork. Then, till he was a teenager, I took up projects with an urban focus, so I didn't need to travel far.

So yes, I did make some compromises and adjust a bit but I'm happy I made those choices. Everyone has challenges and constraints. The trick and the joy is being able to say, okay, how do I take the opportunities I have to the fullest and make my life something that's really meaningful and fulfilling.

Advice to Young Women

70% of my team is female. All very well educated, competent and committed. But they also happily display their feminine side when they come into office. They don't feel afraid to say, "I'm bringing muffins today" or "I'm going to spend this weekend doing crocheting". At the same time we have a young girl who rides an Enfield Bullet.

So, don't box yourself into some particular image, or larger cultural narrative. Be true to yourself, be multidimensional. And remember, in the social sector, needles on the ground don't move very fast. So if you choose this path, be honest, be patient.

AWARDS & HONOURS

- Jim Dooge Award 2015 issued by European Geophysical Union.
- Editors Choice Award 2013 issued by American Geophysical Union.

SPACE MOM

Aerospace is high tech but it is also a place where people understand family situations.

Early Life

I grew up in a lower middle class Kannada speaking family. My dad was in the post and telegraph department, so he would get transferred every 4-5 years. He was determined that we kids should receive a good education. Daddy didn't care whether it was a boy or girl, it was like, you've got to do your best.

He asked for a transfer to Pune when I was in my higher secondary, because it was known for excellence in education at that time. My brother and I were very close, he is just a year younger than me. Both of us were extremely focused on education. That's all I can remember. We didn't do too much else, didn't go anywhere, didn't hang out with friends.

So that's how I made it to IIT Bombay. Honestly, I think it was just hard work and determination. Maths was my strength and my father really encouraged me and demanded perfection, as much as possible. And then I started demanding it of myself. I suppose that's how I became the first female recipient of the gold medal at IIT Bombay.

Life at IIT Bombay

I really enjoyed hanging out with the women in my wing. Otherwise, my focus was only on studies. I didn't really talk to the boys in my class, so it was a bit isolating. I also remember being harassed by a guy who was working in the department, he used to follow me around. The security officer, a family friend, somehow managed to make that person stop.

I didn't think seriously about going abroad until maybe the fifth year. It was only when a close friend of my father insisted I must get the best education possible in the United States. My mom was not very happy about a

DR. VIJAYA KORWAR GALLAGHER

B.Tech, Electrical Engineering, 1976

Chief Architect - Space Segment, Globalstar
Advisor, Sky Quantum

"Make sure your fundamentals are strong."

Gallagher family at daughter Shamala's wedding in Athens, GA

With IIT B classmates during Distinguished Alumnus visit to IIT

young, unmarried girl going to study in a foreign land but dad overruled her. That's how I came to Caltech in Pasadena, California.

Professional Journey

The legendary Prof. John Pierce was my advisor at Caltech. His areas of work included radio communications and microwave technology. It was under his leadership that the first communications satellite, the Telstar, was developed. So 'Picture quality in Synthetic Aperture Radar Imaging' became the subject of my PhD.

> **IIT BOMBAY, TO ME IS: WHERE I LEARNED ALL OF MY FIRST PRINCIPLES IN THE SCIENCES.**

Caltech has very close relationships with the Jet Propulsion Lab, JPL. So I used to work at JPL during the summer and even during the school year, related to my thesis. After my PhD, I worked for JPL for a year. and I got married to a fellow graduate student, Tim Gallagher. I was brought up very conservatively and it was not easy to explain it to my parents.

When Tim moved to San Jose, I started working at Ford Aerospace. Over the course of my career, I developed

RAPID FIRE

If I could: I would have studied a little bit more humanities when I was younger.
I love: Hiking and American football. Strange combination.
The world needs: More women to reach their potential and be encouraged to do that.
I'm passionate about: Understanding what makes people tick.

and managed proposals for commercial satellite operators worldwide. I worked with organisations like Ford Aerospace, Space Systems Loral and Globalstar in key technical leadership positions.

The best part of my career at Globalstar in 2011 (before I went to Loral) was to be the Program Director for the second generation of Globalstar satellites. I spent 6 memorable weeks at Baikonur Cosmodrome for the launch of those satellites.

Work-Life Balance

When I had my first child, my daughter, I decided to stop working. My husband was very supportive. He said, do whatever you want, I earn enough to maintain a decent lifestyle. My son was born three years later. So I was at home with the kids for close to seven years. At best, 1 I did some part time consulting, 8 or 10 hours a month.

I was lucky to be able to go back to the same company. Aerospace is a high tech profession, but it is also a place where people understand family situations. Even back then, they were accepting of the fact that I took some time off. When I was transitioning back, I had this remote terminal which allowed me to work from home. This was pre-internet and felt magical!

My husband and I got divorced after 27 years of marriage. My kids were grown up by then and I was able to travel, for instance, to Baikonur for 6 weeks at a time, without feeling like I was missing out on any responsibilities at home.

Advice to Young Women

If you want to work in space, you probably want to get a Master's or PhD in that area. But I've seen so many people who are not even technical succeed in the satellite world. People stumble into it through operations or programming and learn on the job. So don't be so hung up on what you study.

If you're interested in a field for whatever reason, it catches your eye, even if it's later in your career, go ahead and explore it. Just make sure your fundamentals are strong.

AWARDS & HONORS

- Gold Medallist, IIT Bombay (1976)
- Distinguished Alumna Awardee, IIT Bombay (2005)
- Small Business Innovation Research Award, US Air Force

SWEET MEMORIES

SWEET MEMORIES